This is a continuation in the series of publications produced by the Center for Advanced Concepts and Technology (ACT), which was created as a "skunk works" with funding provided by the CCRP under the auspices of the Assistant Secretary of Defense (C3I). This program has demonstrated the importance of having a research program focused on the national security implications of the Information Age. It develops the theoretical foundations to provide DoD with information superiority and highlights the importance of active outreach and dissemination initiatives designed to acquaint senior military personnel and civilians with these emerging issues. The CCRP Publication Series is a key element of this effort.

Check our Web site for the latest CCRP activities and publications.

www.dodccrp.org

DoD Command and Control Research Program

ASSISTANT SECRETARY OF DEFENSE (NII)
&
CHIEF INFORMATION OFFICER

Dr. Linton Wells, II (Acting)

PRINCIPAL DEPUTY ASSISTANT SECRETARY OF DEFENSE (NII)

Dr. Linton Wells, II

SPECIAL ASSISTANT TO THE ASD(NII)
&
DIRECTOR OF RESEARCH

Dr. David S. Alberts

Library of Congress Cataloging-in-Publication Data

Understanding information age warfare / David S. Alberts ... [et al.].
   p. cm.
  Includes bibliographical references and index.
  ISBN 1-893723-04-6 (pbk.)
   1. Information warfare. 2. Electronics in military engineering--United States. 3. Military planning--United States. I. Alberts, David S. (David Stephen), 1942-
U163 .U49 2001
355.3'43--dc21

                     2001043080

1st printing August 2001
2nd printing July 2002
3rd printing October 2004

UNDERSTANDING INFORMATION AGE WARFARE

David S. Alberts
John J. Garstka
Richard E. Hayes
David T. Signori

Table of Contents

List of Figures

Acknowledgments

This book was, in a very real sense, a community effort. When the CCRP sponsored the formation of the Information Superiority Metrics Working Group (ISMWG) in early 2000, it was our hope that the collegial exchanges would take the discussion of Information Superiority and Network Centric Warfare to the next level—a level where these ideas could be rigorously tested both analytically and experimentally. We are very pleased that this turned out to be the case.

This book attempts to capture, for a wider audience, the insights, suggestions, and discussions that have occurred both at an ISMWG workshop and the regular monthly meetings of the ISMWG. The list of contributors to this book, the members of the ISMWG, are listed on the following page. It should be noted that the ISMWG is a volunteer organization, and as such its very existence is due to the generosity of both the individual members and the organizations for which they work. It should be recognized that the time devoted by ISMWG members is above and beyond their already formidable obligations, both professional and personal. We know that we speak not only for ourselves but also for the community when we express our sincere appreciation for their contributions. The subject addressed by this book is a difficult one, and contributions will be required from all of us if we are to continue to make progress.

We owe a huge debt of thanks to John McDaniel for working with us to develop the annotated briefing which served to solidify our thoughts, and to Margita

Rushing for her work to turn this into a polished manuscript and prepare it for the printers.

Finally, the authors deeply appreciate the opportunity to write this book. We hope we have done justice to the deliberations of the ISMWG and that in extending these we have added to an understanding of this challenging subject.

Information Superiority Metrics Working Group (ISMWG)

Dave Alberts, OSD	Tom Altshuler, DARPA
David Anhalt, OSD	James Baxfield, IDA
Bill Bowling, OPNAV/N6C	Dan de Mots, BAH
John Dickman, NWC	Gary Edwards, ISX
Ward Evans, MITRE	Marco Fiorello, SYYS
Colleen Gagnon, Metron	John Garstka, Joint Staff
Greg Giovanis, DISA	Priscilla Glasow, MITRE
Ray Haller, MITRE	Tim Hanley, Joint Staff
Dick Hayes, EBR	Paul Hiniker, DISA
Joseph Jennings, MITRE	Hans Keithley, OSD
Mike Letsky, ONR	Cliff Lieberman, JFCOM
Julia Loughran, ThoughtLink	Mark Mandeles, J. de Bloch
Geoffrey Maron, AFSAA/SAAI	Ken McGruther, WBB
Donald McSwain, SYYS	John Mills, JFCOM
Greg Parnell, Toffler Associates	Ed Peartree, OSD
Peter Perla, CNA	Dennis Popiela, JFCOM
Todd Riebel, OSD	Steve Rudder, OSD
Dave Signori, RAND	Ed Smith, Boeing
Stephen Soules, BAH	Fred Stein, MITRE
Bill Stevens, Metron	Stu Starr, MITRE
Joe Tatman, Litton TASC	Chuck Taylor, OSD
Mark Tempestilli, OPNAV/N6C	Gary Toth, ONR
Gerald Tunnicliff, NSA	Frank Vaughan, JHU/APL
Gary Wheatley, EBR	Larry Wiener, OPNAV/N6C
Doug Williams, Litton TASC	

Preface

Understanding the Emerging Theory of Warfare

The age we live in is full of contradictions. It is a time unlike any other, a time when the pace of change demands that we change while we are still at the top of our game in order to survive the next wave. It is a time when our analysis methods are becoming less and less able to shed light on the choices we face. It is a time when the tried and true approaches to military command and control, organization, and doctrine need to be re-examined.

Fortunately, we are not alone. Organizations in every competitive space and individuals in every area of human endeavor are grappling with the relentless demands of our age. In the private sector, Darwinian principles are ruthlessly at work. Organizational genetics are producing mutations that are being mercilessly tested in the marketplace. Evolution is about the adaptation of the species through competitive selection. Individual organisms are not expected to adapt; rather those organisms that survive pass on their proven or adapted genetic material to the next generation.

Industries are like species in that they can adapt as a whole, even as many individual organizations fail, are merged, and are acquired. The role of militaries as they relate to national security and the way militaries will be organized and equipped will undoubtedly undergo transformation as they adapt to the Information Age. While each of us harbors some idea about how militaries will respond to a myriad of Information Age pressures, it is safe to say that there will be surprises along the way. Progress will not be orderly, nor will it be predictable. This will be hard for many to understand and accept. Cherished notions of long-range planning and ways of introducing new technology are arguably outdated.

This book presents an alternative to the deterministic and linear strategies of the planning modernization that are now an artifact of the Industrial Age. The approach being advocated here begins with the premise that adaptation to the Information Age centers around the ability of an organization or an individual to utilize information. This book identifies what this deceptively simple Information Age characteristic actually entails and how learning to use information is an inherently complex and disruptive process. It argues that innovation, discovery, and experimentation are fundamental Information Age competencies. Given the dynamics and complexities of our time and the incredible pace of change, planning is truly—as the old adage goes—all about the process, not the plan.

If this book helps you understand why Information Superiority and network-centric concepts are at the heart of all Information Age organizations, challenges the way you think about the future of DoD, provides you with an idea or two about how to capitalize on the information we have or could have, or simply makes you think again about how we change, it will have accomplished what the authors set out to do.

CHAPTER 1

Introduction

Background

Armed with a general understanding of the concepts of Information Superiority and Network Centric Warfare, enterprising individuals and organizations are developing new ways of accomplishing their missions by leveraging the power of information and applying network-centric concepts. Visions are being created and significant progress is being made. But to date we have been only scratching the surface of what is possible. A great deal of what has been done is "picking low-hanging fruit" by direct application of new technology with existing practice. Progress is also "hit and miss," in that progress has not been systematic or achieved across the board. Hence we have only begun to take advantage of the opportunities afforded by rapidly advancing information technology. There are a number of reasons for this. Two stand out. First, there is the complexity of the task. This involves being able to deal with the coevolution of mission capability packages consisting of a concept of operations, approach to command and control, organization, doctrine, corresponding C4ISR, weapons, and logistics systems. Second is the lack of maturity of our understanding of basics of Information Superiority and Network Centric Warfare.

Progress in science and its application to a domain always involves a mutually re-enforcing spiral of theory and practice. With respect to Information Superiority and Network Centric Warfare, we are still in the initial spiral. For many, Information Superiority and Network Centric Warfare remain abstract concepts, their applicability to military operations and organizations unclear, and their value unproven. Others have seen the benefits but are unable to adequately "connect the dots" between improved information (and/or its distribution) and outcomes in a rigorous (scientifically rigorous, meaning both valid and reliable) way.

Moving into the next spiral requires that we improve our understanding of how Information Superiority is created and how Network Centric Warfare concepts can translate Information Superiority into increased combat power and military effectiveness. Accomplishing this requires progress in three specific areas. First, we need to articulate the key concepts underlying Information Superiority and Network Centric Warfare and the ways they are interrelated. Second, we need to be able to measure the degree to which these concepts are realized. Third, we need to be able to systematically explore the relationships between the realization of key concepts and the conduct and results of military operations.

Purpose

The purpose of this book is to contribute to our ability to move to the next spiral by providing a more detailed articulation of Information Superiority and Network Centric Warfare. Toward this end, this book proposes working definitions, defines the specific characteristics and the attributes of key concepts, specifies (and hypothesizes) the relationships among them, and offers ways to measure the degree to which these concepts are realized and the impact they have on the conduct and effectiveness of military operations.

Foundations of Understanding

As the title of this book is *Understanding Information Age Warfare*, it is fitting that we begin with a discussion about the nature of understanding and the necessary processes and tools to achieve it.

Nature of Understanding

Developing an understanding of how and why things work as they do, or could work, is fundamental to being able to systematically improve functionality. Without such an understanding, progress will continue to be a hit or miss proposition. Understanding enables us to focus attention on making those changes that are most promising.

The initial journey on the road to understanding is haphazard, characterized by fits and starts. The first real sign of progress involves the emergence and acceptance of a special language to describe and talk about the problem. This language identifies and defines the primitives needed to build a theory. It enables meaningful discussions and comparisons.

Next, the theory coalesces. The initial articulation of the theory identifies and describes the relationships that are hypothesized to exist among the primitives. The theory may be quite profound, even if there are only a small number of primitives (e.g., $E = mc^2$).

Theories are merely unproven conjectures (or perhaps sets of related, but untested, hypotheses). They need to be tested. Sometimes this is very difficult, as it was with Einstein's theory of relativity. To test a theory (or an integrated set of hypotheses), the primitives must be clearly defined and measured. Measurement requires two things: a definition of what is to be measured (validity), and instruments capable of measuring it consistently (reliability).

Progress Toward Understanding

Developing an understanding of the complex relationships among information quality, knowledge, awareness, the degree to which information is shared, shared awareness, the nature of collaboration, and its effect on synchronization, and turning this understanding into deployed military capability, requires an iterative process. At this point in time we have a highly immature notion (concept or model) of how these primitives are interrelated and the nature of the effects they have on the accomplishment of military tasks. The existence of a set of primitives and a set of integrated hypotheses about the inter-relationships satisfies the minimum specifications for a conceptual framework or model. With the first instance of a model, we can now begin a process that will mature our model and with it our understanding, thereby enabling us to more systematically field improved operational capabilities.

However, we cannot afford to wait until we develop a full understanding of how information and networking can be leveraged before fielding new and improved mission capability packages for two reasons. The first is that we should take advantage of our existing understanding (however limited) to make significant low-risk improvements. The second reason really goes to the heart of the scientific process. We will never develop a complete understanding unless we learn from practical experience and empirical observation. Hence we need to field capabilities so that we can learn to improve them. This is not a problem that can be completely solved in a laboratory, but rather one that will require a tremendous amount of interaction between theory and practice. Humans are central to the problem, and we have no fully valid and reliable models that will allow us to forecast human and organizational behaviors. Even if we had such models, the military arena is so complex and the number of relevant factors so large that we could not account for all of them in any set of models or simulations. Hence, we must find practical, empirical approaches in order to advance understanding and turn ideas into useful systems and practices.

From Theory to Practice

The spiral shown in Figure 1 illustrates the efforts involved in getting one application of the theory into practice. Just as the theory evolves iteratively as a result of incorporating the learning from research and experimental activities and feedback from applications, so each application of the theory should go through a spiral development process of its own.

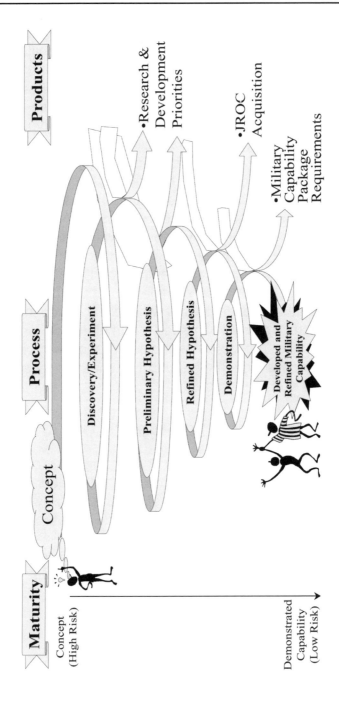

Figure 1. From Theory to Practice

The application starts as a concept for a mission capability package identifying the (a) concept for way the operation will be conducted; (b) the command and control approach to be employed; (c) the relevant organization and doctrine, collaborative arrangements, and information flows; (d) the nature of the education and training required; and (e) the specification of the forces and assets. The important thing to note is that this initial version of the concept is only a point of departure for a series of discovery experiments that will help us explore ways to make the basic idea behind the concept work.

Out of this series of discovery experiments will come a set of preliminary hypotheses that will serve as the drivers for a series of experiments designed to test them. Several series of experiments may be necessary to sort out all of the issues involved. Ultimately, a successful concept (as modified and refined) may be demonstrated. Along the way some concepts and processes will be eliminated. Others will be found applicable only under some circumstances.

Once the concept has been successfully demonstrated, it is ready to be implemented. The advantage of this spiral process is that it serves to coevolve each of the elements of the mission capability package so that these work together synergistically.

With this overview of the process that takes us from theory to practice in mind, we will now turn our attention back to the beginning—the development of a language with which to construct a theory of Information Superiority and Network Centric Warfare.

Organization of Book

This volume began with a discussion of the foundations of understanding, which is followed by introductory material on the language of Information Superiority and Network Centric Warfare. The book goes on to discuss the fundamental role of information in warfare, as well as what is different in Information Age command, control, communications, and intelligence (C3I). The fundamental concepts of Information Superiority and Network Centric Warfare are explored next, followed by a discussion of the three domains where C3I occurs: the physical domain, the information domain, and the cognitive domain. This is followed by consideration of the key arenas of awareness, shared awareness, collaborative planning, and synchronized actions. Applications of these theories are discussed next, including summaries of key portions of the accumulating body of evidence that demonstrate the importance and impact of Information Age approaches. Finally, a brief assessment of the state of the art and practice is used to introduce key ideas about the way ahead—how we can move from a better understanding of Information Age Warfare towards its effective practice.

CHAPTER 2

The Language of Information Age Warfare

The Language of Information Superiority and Network Centric Warfare

C reating a special language that allows us to express our ideas about Information Age Warfare concepts in somewhat precise and unambiguous terms is a necessary prerequisite to useful discourse and meaningful exploration. For example, as we write this, definitions of Information Superiority abound. Each one is an attempt to convey some important aspect or facet of this complex concept. This multiplicity of definitions can be frustrating. There have been many calls for a definitive statement of what Information Superiority really means. We would suggest that this is and needs to be a work in progress. The first order of business is to develop a useful language that contains the basic ideas from which a deeper understanding of Information Superiority and Network Centric Warfare can be built. That is not to say that we will refrain from offering our view of what

Information Superiority means, expressed in the language that we develop here, but that we consider these definitions to be points of departure rather than etched in stone.

In this section we introduce the domains that are central to an understanding of the nature and impact of information and a set of primitives that define the building blocks from which an indepth understanding of Information Superiority and Network Centric Warfare can be developed.

The Domains

To understand how information affects our ability to perform military operations it is necessary to think about three domains—the physical domain, the information domain, and the cognitive domain.[1]

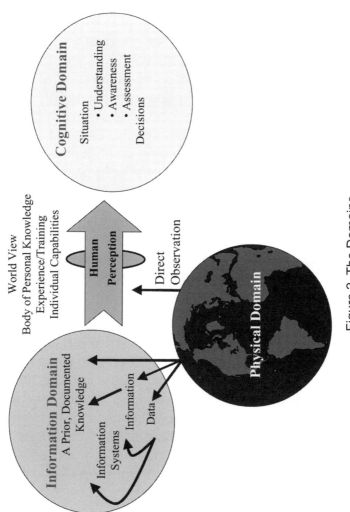

Figure 2. The Domains

The physical domain is the place where the situation the military seeks to influence exists. It is the domain where strike, protect, and maneuver take place across the environments of ground, sea, air, and space.[2] It is the domain where physical platforms and the communications networks that connect them reside. Comparatively, the elements of this domain are the easiest to measure, and consequently, combat power has traditionally been measured primarily in this domain. In our analyses and models, the physical domain is characterized as reality, or ground truth. Important metrics for measuring combat power in this domain include lethality and survivability.

The information domain is where information lives. It is the domain where information is created, manipulated, and shared. It is the domain that facilitates the communication of information among warfighters. It is the domain where the command and control of modern military forces is communicated, where commander's intent is conveyed.

The information that exists in the information domain may or may not truly reflect ground truth. For example, a sensor observes the real world and produces an output (data) which exists in the information domain. With the exception of direct sensory observation, all of our information about the world comes through and is affected by our interaction with the information domain. And it is through the information domain that we communicate with others (telepathy would be an exception).

Consequently, it is increasingly the information domain that must be protected and defended to enable a force to generate combat power in the face of offensive actions taken by an adversary. And, in the all important battle for Information Superiority, the information domain is ground zero.

The cognitive domain is in the minds of the participants. This is the place where perceptions, awareness, understanding, beliefs, and values reside and where, as a result of sensemaking, decisions are made. This is the domain where many battles and wars are actually won and lost. This the domain of intangibles: leadership, morale, unit cohesion, level of training and experience, situational awareness, and public opinion. This is the domain where an understanding of commander's intent, doctrine, tactics, techniques, and procedures reside. Much has been written about this domain, and key attributes of this domain have remained relatively constant since Sun Tzu wrote *The Art of War*. The attributes of this domain are extremely difficult to measure, and each sub-domain (each individual mind) is unique.

Note that *all* of the contents of the cognitive domain pass through a filter or lens we have labeled human perception. This filter consists of the individual's worldview, the body of personal knowledge the person brings to the situation, their experience, training, values, and individual capabilities (intelligence, personal style, perceptual capabilities, etc.). Since these human perceptual lenses are unique to each individual, we know that individual cognition (understandings, etc.) are also unique. There is one reality, or physical domain. This is converted into selected data, information, and knowledge by the systems in the information domain. By training and shared experience we try to make the cognitive activities of military decisionmakers similar, but they nevertheless remain unique to each individual, with differences being more significant among individuals from different Services, generations, and countries than they are among individuals from the same unit or Service.

Primitives

We have identified a relatively small number of primitives that are needed to develop a theory of how information affects the performance of individuals and organizations. These primitives are:

Sensing	Awareness	Decisions
Observations (data)	Understanding	Actions
Information	Sharing	Synchronization
Knowledge	Collaboration	

Each of these primitives will be defined and depicted graphically in relationship to the three domains. This depiction is useful because it forces us to think about where (in which domain(s)) one must measure a particular primitive.

Sensing

Two modes of sensing are portrayed in Figure 3: direct sensing and indirect sensing.

Direct sensing takes place when humans experience an object or event in the physical domain with one of their senses (such as seeing, hearing, or smelling), and the sensing registers directly in the cognitive domain. Indirect sensing takes place when a sensor of some type is employed by a human to facilitate sensing some aspect of the physical domain.

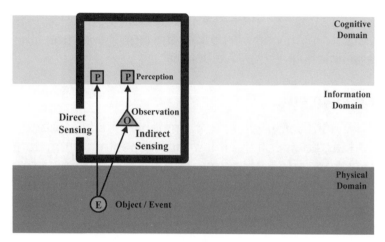

Figure 3. Domain Relationships: Sensing

This figure portrays indirect sensing as being mapped from the physical domain onto the information domain, and passing through the information domain before it is filtered by human perception. Direct sensing is shown as a mapping from the physical domain directly into the cognitive domain.

For thousands of years, direct sensing was the primary mode of gathering information about the battlefield. Starting in the 17th century, direct sensing was facilitated by technology in the form of telescopes and field glasses. In World War II, new sensors, in the forms of radio detection and ranging (radar), and sound detection and ranging (sonar) were employed. These greatly increased the ability to see the battlefield and reduce uncertainty with respect to the position of airplanes and submarines which where virtually invisible before. Today, we use a rich suite of sensors (night vision goggles, heat sensors, satellite technologies, etc.) to help us sense the battlespace. When technology is used to extract data, it forms part of the information domain. An observation, or data item, is created. This data is perceived only after it passes through the human filter and enters the cognitive domain.

Information

The word *information* is commonly used to refer to various points on the information spectrum from data to knowledge. However, as a primitive term, information is the result of putting individual observations (sensor returns or data items) into some *meaningful context.*

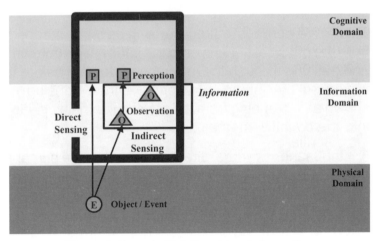

Figure 4. Domain Relationships: Information

Data is a representation of individual facts, concepts, or instructions in a manner suitable for communication, interpretation, or processing by humans or by automatic means. Examples of data include radar returns, sensor reports, and recorded observations. The term *processed* data is often used, though, in fact, all data is processed. When this term is used it is meant to imply additional processing. Note that information is created whenever indirect sensing is used. As the figure illustrates, some observations may be lost, left inside the information domain, or filtered out by the perceptual lenses of individuals.

Knowledge

Knowledge involves conclusions drawn from *patterns* suggested by available information. Knowledge of the situation results from conclusions that can be drawn from information about, for example, the types and locations of battlespace entities.

Knowledge exists in both the information and the cognitive domains. Some knowledge is pre-existing. For example, doctrine is often a means of fitting together information about a situation and the appropriate or desired actions given that situation. Knowledge is accumulated in the cognitive domain as the result of learning and is stored in the information domain where it is potentially widely available.

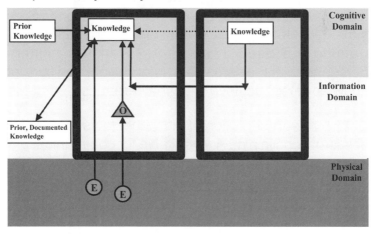

Figure 5. Domain Relationships: Knowledge

Knowledge can be loaded into the cognitive domain of an individual via several possible paths, including:

1. previous education, training, or experience

2. direct experience with the physical domain

3. interaction with other humans

4. interaction with the information domain

Knowledge can also be mapped from the cognitive domain into the information domain, which occurs when it is being transferred to other humans, as instructions or rules to machines, or for storage and retrieval in computers.

Awareness

Awareness exists in the cognitive domain. Awareness relates to a situation and, as such, is the result of a complex interaction between prior knowledge (and beliefs) and current perceptions of reality. Each individual has a unique awareness of any given military situation. Here, again, professional education and training are used in an effort to ensure military personnel with the same data, information, and current knowledge will achieve similar awareness.

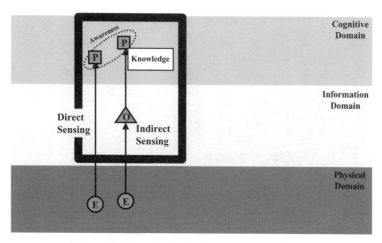

Figure 6. Domain Relationships: Awareness

Understanding

Understanding involves having a sufficient level of knowledge to be able to draw inferences about the possible consequences of the situation, as well as sufficient awareness of the situation to predict future patterns. Hence, situation awareness focuses on what is known about past and present situations, while understanding of a military situation focuses on what the situation is becoming (or can become) and how different actions will impact the emerging situation.

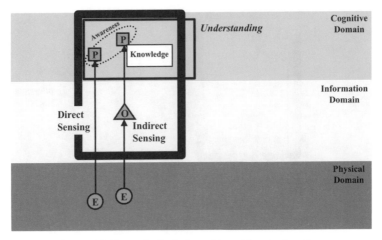

Figure 7. Domain Relationships: Understanding

Decisions

Decisions also take place in the cognitive domain. They are choices about what is to be done. Decisions are acted upon and/or conveyed via the information domain for others to act upon, resulting in or influencing actions in the physical domain and/or other decisions. While they occur at all levels in the organization, the emphasis traditionally has been focused on headquarters' decisions. In order to adequately explore Information Age concepts, we will need to expand our view of decisions to include all those that significantly affect battlefield outcomes. For example, orders may tell a force what to do, where to do it, and when to do it. A decision to assign a new mission to subordinate forces may, in contrast, cause that organization to undertake new decision processes. On the other hand, subordinates may implement a commander's intent (not explicit command decisions) by making a series of decisions.

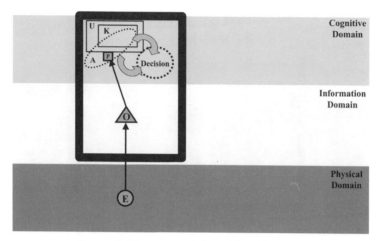

Figure 8. Domain Relationships: Decision

Although decisions are depicted here as a result of an understanding,[3] decisions can obviously be made absent any understanding. However, such decisions would essentially be random rather than purposeful and would, therefore, be unlikely to prove effective in a military context. We assume here that military commanders and the forces they command (the individuals we are concerned about) will always possess some level of knowledge and some level of situational awareness. Implicitly, therefore, they have situational understanding and their decisions are purposeful.

Actions

Actions take place in the physical domain. They are triggered by decisions in the cognitive domain that either are directly translated into action or have been transported through the information domain to others. This figure portrays an individual's state of knowledge as influencing the state of awareness, situation understanding, and the decisionmaking process. This diagram also highlights awareness of a specific situation as an input to the decisionmaking process.

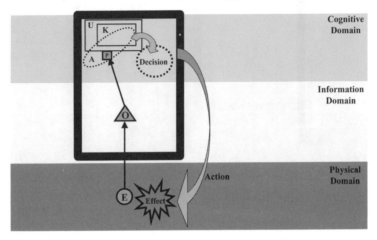

Figure 9. Domain Relationships: Action

Figure 10 portrays the *observe-orient-decide-act* (OODA) loop.[4] Boyd developed and initially applied the concept in an attempt to understand how a competitive advantage could be achieved by pilots engaged in air-to-air combat. Boyd's initial application of the OODA loop was to a platform-centric warfighting environment, where he observed that the speed with which a pilot moves through the OODA process can serve as a source of competitive advantage. He developed this insight by trying to understand all the factors that contributed to the 10-to-1 kill ratio that American pilots flying F-86s were able to establish over their North Korean and Chinese adversaries flying MiG-15s.[5] The OODA is a sequential process and reflects neither the way experts are thought to make decisions, nor the way collaborative decisions are made.[6]

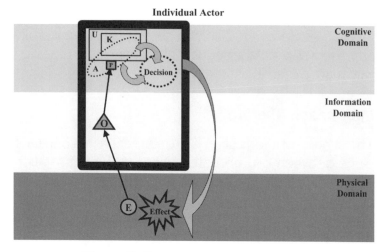

Figure 10. Example: Entity OODA Loop

The OODA loop is most applicable for direct action, action which is taken by the decisionmaker. In fact, it is useful to make distinctions between different kinds of decisions. Simple decisions are those that involve a selection from a set of options with the simplest ones involving whether to act (e.g., shoot) or not. Complex decisions involve the development of a set of options, the criteria for choosing among them, and the combination of rules by which those criteria are integrated. For example developing, assessing, and selecting courses of action at the Joint Task Force level is generally a complex decision. This distinction is important in understanding future C3I and how it must be supported. It is developed in more detail later.

For many simple decisions the OODA loop is short-circuited because observations may be mapped directly onto decision options. The application of network-centric concepts changes both the topology of decisions an organization makes and the kinds of decisions (simple or complex) that are made. Hence the term *operating inside the enemy OODA loop* cannot be taken literally as we move to replace sequential planning and execution with more dynamic alternatives.

Information Sharing

The sharing of information is an interaction that can take place between two or more entities in the information domain. These could be between humans, databases, or programs such as planning or fire control applications. The ability to share information is key to being able to develop a state of shared awareness, as well as being able to collaborate and/or synchronize.

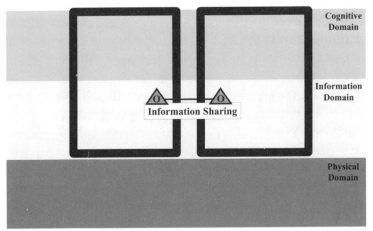

Figure 11. Domain Relationships: Information Sharing

This diagram describes an interaction between entities where information is exchanged. The concept of sharing extends, or course, beyond two entities. Any number of entities may be involved and the form of the sharing can vary significantly. This theme is also treated in greater detail later.

When two or more people are located in close proximity, information can be exchanged by voice via face-to-face conversation. Other techniques that employ body movement, such as hand signals, can also be employed. Body language can also be used to communicate information, but it is easy to miss or misunderstand these signals. In some cases, visual aids can also be used to enhance ideas or concepts of communication.

When two or more people are geographically separated, some type of technology must be employed to share information (e.g., telephone, e-mail, video teleconferencing). Over time, various types and kinds of technologies have been developed to capture, store, and transmit information. As is discussed in detail later, information technology defines the boundaries and capabilities of the information domain.

Shared Knowledge

Shared knowledge exists to some degree in all human efforts to work together. However, the extent of this sharing varies dramatically. Training and doctrine have been employed throughout history to develop a high degree of shared knowledge among troops so that they will understand and react to situations in a predictable way. This predictability is essential so independent elements of a force can coordinate their actions. It becomes vital when forces attempt to coordinate their actions without communications or attempt self-synchronization.

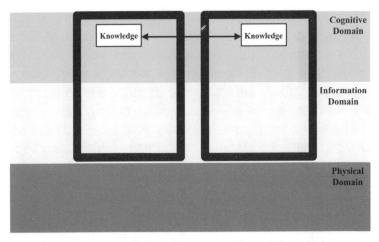

Figure 12. Domain Relationships: Shared Knowledge

The degree to which shared knowledge can be developed has a significant influence on the nature of command and control that can be employed, the nature and amount of communications that are needed to develop and maintain shared awareness, and the ease and degree to which forces can be synchronized.

Shared Awareness

Shared awareness is a state that exists in the cognitive domain when two or more entities are able to develop a similar awareness of a situation. The degree of similarity required (or difference tolerable) will depend on the type and degree of collaboration and synchronization needed.

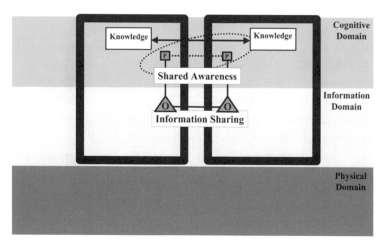

Figure 13. Domain Relationships: Shared Awareness

Multiple factors influence the degree to which a state of shared awareness can be developed between two or more entities. These certainly include the degree of shared information and knowledge, but are also heavily influenced by similarities and differences in worldview, culture, language, and perceived interests. Shared awareness is an important prerequisite for the ability to synchronize actions in the physical domain in the absence of a detailed plan.

Measuring a state of shared awareness is more complex than measuring a state of shared information. It cannot be measured directly. Rather, it must be measured and assessed indirectly based on observable behaviors and direct questioning of subjects.

Collaboration

Collaboration is a process that takes place between two or more entities. Collaboration always implies working together toward a common purpose. This distinguishes it from simply sharing data, information, knowledge, or awareness. It is also a process that takes place in the cognitive domain. In Figure 14, the collaboration process is represented as a dotted box between two entities. Collaboration requires the ability to share information. One of the key benefits of a network-centric environment is the ability to share information and collaborate over distance.

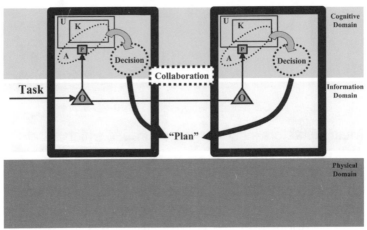

Figure 14. Domain Relationships: Collaboration

Synchronization

Synchronization takes place in the physical domain (reality). Synchronization is the meaningful arrangement of things or effects in time and space. Such synchronization can be the result of detailed planning and conscious coordination or collaboration. However, it can also result from shared situational awareness that provides an adequate guideline for action. The detailed orchestration of *Operation Overlord* and other Allied plans during World War II are excellent examples of formal synchronization. The simple practice of "marching to the sound of the guns" in 19th century warfare is an example of guidelines that enabled commanders to support one another, or synchronize their actions, without detailed prior coordination.

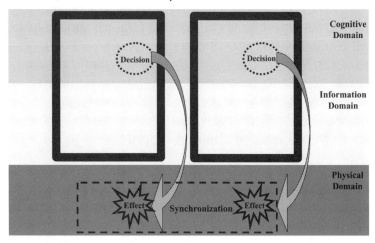

Figure 15. Domain Relationships: Synchronization

Summary of Primitives

This completes the introduction of the set of primitives from which the concepts that lie at the heart of Information Superiority and Network Centric Warfare can be constructed. As noted earlier, this discussion makes the language used in the rest of the volume explicit. The authors remain open to better ideas or more useful definitions. In order to make these primitives useful, however, we need to explain more about them, particularly how they can be observed and measured. A discussion of metrics will set the stage for more detailed discussions about the primitives and the relationships between them.

Role of Metrics

Each of the primitives introduced in the previous chapter has a set of attributes associated with it that help us measure its value (e.g., information quality) or the degree to which it is realized (e.g., degree of synchronization). Each of these attributes represents a feature or characteristic that is important in understanding the nature, impacts, and/or value of information. Latency, for example, is an attribute of information.

A metric is a standard of measurement: measuring specifically the dimensions, capacity, quantity, or other characteristic of an attribute so that comparisons can be made. Hence, without a set of metrics associated with the primitives, we do not have a standard means of measuring and comparing their characteristics. Without a standard way of measuring attributes of interest, we cannot link theory to practice. We would not be able therefore to trace an effect back to a cause or set of conditions necessary and sufficient to achieve an effect.

This describes the current state of affairs all too well. In the experiments that the community has run so far, a number of technical capabilities are introduced that are hypothesized to have some effect on the way individuals and organizations behave, which in turn is hypothesized to impact performance positively. These experiments are almost universally declared successes. However, because we were not able to instrument them fully, we cannot know exactly what happened or why. This greatly limits the usefulness of these events and squanders opportunities to contribute to our understanding of how information can be effectively leveraged.

Hierarchy of Measures

Figure 16 depicts the primitives in the context of a hierarchy of measures that can be employed to understand the Information Superiority/Network Centric Warfare value chain. Neither Information Superiority nor Network Centric Warfare are ends unto themselves. Their value depends upon the impact they have on military tasks and missions. This hierarchy consists of four bands of measures: richness, reach, command and control (C2), and value. The measures in each band address a key portion of the value chain. The first band, richness, contains measures that address the quality of the information content as it exists in both the information and cognitive domains. These measures, in effect, can be used to tell us if this is the right information. The second band, reach, contains measures that focus on the ability of an organization to share information and develop shared awareness. These measures assess whether or not we are getting the information to the right people. They also reflect how well individuals are being educated and trained, the quality of information sharing, and the collaborative processes designed to help develop a common perception of the situation. The third band, command and control, measures the products of a command and control process—the quality of the decisions that are made and the synchronization that is achieved. Finally, the fourth band provides measures that address the bottom line value of information-related capabilities; that is, the ability to accomplish military missions and to use that military mission effectiveness to achieve policy success.

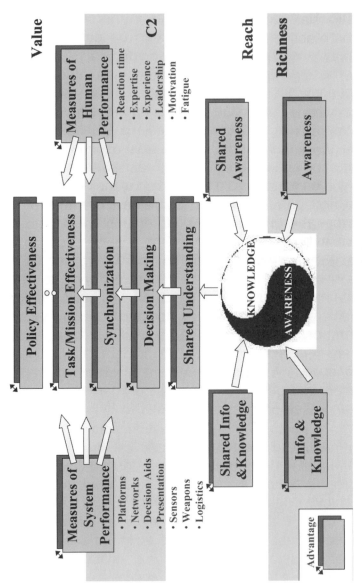

Figure 16. Hierarchy of Measures

This hierarchy of measures is more comprehensive than the measures that have been traditionally used in C4ISR-related studies, analyses, and models. The state of the practice employs system performance and/or rudimentary measures of information quality that are hypothesized to be directly linked to task and mission performance. No attempt is normally made to instrument or parameterize the intermediate links in the chain. Issues related to how information may be perceived, what prior knowledge might exist, and how information sharing affects the process are not usually addressed. These are but a few of the many factors which affect the nature of the impact that information has on the battlespace. Without explicit consideration of all of the important links in the value chain, it is impossible to state with any authority the circumstances under which information is of value and when it is not. Further, no light is shed on the weak link in the value chain. In point of fact the hypothesis that higher quality information will improve task performance is, in reality, a set of linkage hypotheses that trace the effects and impacts of information quality a link at a time through the hierarchy in Figure 16. Developing an understanding of Information Age Warfare depends upon our ability to trace information-related impacts and relate them to measures of value. This hierarchy provides a point of departure for efforts designed to do just this.

The value of information is, as was pointed out earlier, highly dependent upon its application and circumstances. The search to understand the value of information to warfighters would therefore be greatly aided if we had an appreciation of the role that information has played in warfare and could play in the future. This is the subject of the next chapter.

_____

[1]John J. Garstka, "Network Centric Warfare: An Overview of Emerging Theory," *PHALANX* (December 2000).

[2]Mark Herman, *Measuring the Effects of Network-Centric Warfare*, Vol. 1, technical report prepared for the Director of Net Assessment, Office of the Secretary of Defense (McLean, VA: Booz Allen & Hamilton, April 28, 1999).

[3]Gary Klein, *Sources of Power* (Cambridge: MIT Press, 1998).

[4]Col. John R. Boyd, USAF, *Patterns of Conflict* (Unpublished Lecture, 1977). Col. John R. Boyd, USAF, "A Discourse on Winning and Losing." A collection of unpublished briefings and essays (Maxwell AFB, AL: Air University Library, 1976-1992). http://www.belisarius.com/modern_business_strategy/boyd/essence/eowl_frameset.htm (January 1996).

[5]Franklin C. Spinney, "Genghis John," *Proceedings of the U.S. Naval Institute* (July 1997), pp. 42-47.

[6]Gary Klein, *Sources of Power* (Cambridge: MIT Press, 1998).

CHAPTER 3

Information in Warfare

Information in War: Value of Knowledge

Information has been at the core of military operations through the ages. Throughout history, military leaders have recognized the key role of information as a contributor to victory on the battlefield. Commanders have always sought—and sometimes gained—a decisive information advantage over their adversaries. The writings of both Sun Tzu and Clausewitz reflect the key role of information in warfare. Sun Tzu, writing 2,500 years ago, emphasized the importance of knowledge in war.

Know the enemy and know yourself; in a hundred battles you will never know peril. When you are ignorant of the enemy but know yourself, your chances of winning or losing are equal. If ignorant of both your enemy and yourself, you are certain in every battle to be in peril.

—**Sun Tzu**

Figure 17. Information War: Value of Knowledge

The writings of Carl von Clausewitz are famous for their articulation of the fog and friction of war.

Figure 18. Carl von Clausewitz

The general unreliability of all information presents a special problem: all action takes place, so to speak, in a kind of twilight,...like fog. War is the realm of uncertainty; three quarters of the factors on which action in war is based are wrapped in a fog of greater or lessor uncertainty...The commander must work in a medium which his eyes cannot see, which his best deductive powers cannot always fathom; and which, because of constant changes, he can rarely be familiar.

—From Carl von Clausewitz's *On War*

As a result of this enduring characteristic of war, military organizations have, for centuries, been designed to accommodate the lack of available information, that is, how to deal with the fog of war. Fog is all about uncertainty. Uncertainty about where everyone is, what their capabilities are, and the nature of their intentions.

Until recently a commander could not even have a timely and accurate picture of his own forces let alone be comfortable in his knowledge of where the enemy was and what they were up to.

Friction is all about the glitches that occur in carrying out plans to synchronize forces or even to accomplish the most simple tasks. Some of this friction can be attributed to fog, some to poor communications, and some to a lack of shared knowledge.

To compound the problem, decisionmaking in war carries with it an extremely high cost of error. Therefore, it is not surprising that military concepts of operation, organizations, doctrine, and training have always been preoccupied with reducing the effects and risks associated with fog and friction.

Taken together, these enduring characteristics of war have shaped our traditions, our military culture, and our thinking. Departure from these norms will be difficult and will require a high degree of proof that the new way is not only better, but is also robust.

Recent advances in technology offer an opportunity to reduce fog and friction. However, despite all of the advances that have and will likely be made, significant residual fog and friction will persist. The nature of this residual uncertainly is, as yet, unclear and its implications are not fully understood. Nevertheless, there is an historic opportunity to reconsider how best to deal with the fog and friction that will persist, and this is likely to have profound implications for military operations and organizations.

Impact of Fog and Friction

Figure 19 illustrates the relationship between the amount of fog and friction and the level of synchronization that is likely to be achieved in military operations, which is directly related to effectiveness. For almost all of recorded history, we have operated in various parts of the shaded area depicted in Figure 19, trying to avoid the worst parts of this space (the lower right).

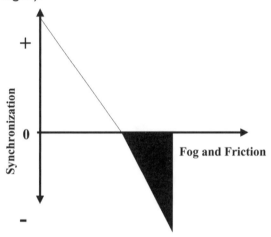

Figure 19. Impact of Fog and Friction on Effectiveness

The Information Age gives us an opportunity to move into the white area. We must recognize that there is a limit to our ability to reduce the fog and friction of war and that in many cases it may not even be possible. We have witnessed the complexity of 21st century missions in Somalia and Bosnia as well as our limitations in being able to collect, process, and distribute needed information for allied air attacks on Belgrade during *Operation Allied Force*.

Hence, our goal in examining the role of information in warfare is to better understand not only how to create and leverage an information advantage, but also how to better deal with the residual uncertainty that will surely exist.

Visionaries who have proclaimed that we will have total awareness or that we will eliminate the fog of war are indeed false prophets—and dangerous ones at that. This is not only for the obvious reason that they could lead some down an unproductive road, but perhaps more importantly, they are poisoning the well for ideas to capitalize on emerging information and networking capabilities that will provide real opportunities to improve our military effectiveness.

Coping with Fog and Friction

As a direct result of the considerable uncertainty, the limits on our ability to effectively communicate on the battlefield, and the very high cost of error, information flows have historically been tied to the command structure and battlefield behaviors were consciously circumscribed and scripted.

Commanders traditionally have dealt with uncertainty through approaches that minimized risks, most notably the risk of being surprised. Success often came to the side that made the least errors, not the side that was imaginative or bold. However, the price for hedging against fog and friction have been high because these solutions carry some significant drawbacks. They lack the ability to exploit opportunities, lack responsiveness, and cannot easily adapt to changing circumstances. They are also highly resource inefficient. In short, these traditional adaptations are 180 degrees out of phase with the desirable attributes of an Information Age military.

Advances in the Information Domain

For the better part of history information processing took place only within the brain and communications were limited to runner, rider, semaphore, drums, or carrier pigeon.

Until recent times, the capability to collect, record, store, process, and disseminate information was extremely limited. Note the relatively similar capabilities that existed in the times of Sun Tzu and Clausewitz in contrast with the dramatically different situation that exists today. The comparative lack of information technology in Sun Tzu's and Clausewitz's times limited the ability of commanders to know what was going on and their ability to communicate and collaborate with their subordinates. These limitations affected the ways in which militaries were able to operate. Even though many advances have taken place, particularly since the introduction of the telegraph in the 19th century, our ability to collect, process, and disseminate information continues to constrain how we operate today.

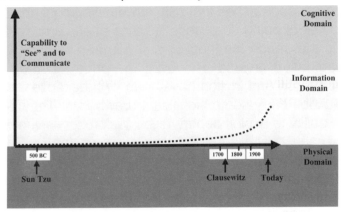

Figure 20. Advances in the Information Capabilities

In the section on command and control we explore the various ways forces have organized, the manner in which command and control has been exercised, and the relationships among organization, command and control, and information and communications technologies. Here we will very briefly review the nature of the advances in information-related technologies, the most significant of which, arguably those related to the Internet, have taken place only in the last 10 years.

Information and the Advantage in Warfare

The chronicles of warfare are replete with examples of victory being denied to the side with the presumed competitive advantage. Analyses of these situations shows that the presumed victor was usually the side with the relative force advantage; that is, an advantage in the physical domain (e.g., numbers, equipment). The causes of these upsets form the basis for much of military education. A contemporary student of warfare knows that these upsets were not upsets at all but the result of a failure to recognize that competitive advantage is not necessarily equivalent to force advantage.

A competitive advantage derives from a synthesis of a critical mass of relative advantages in several arenas: information, knowledge, understanding, decisionmaking (command and control), which are addressed in this book and other arenas including morale and leadership which have been treated extensively elsewhere. A failure to achieve a relative advantage in any one of these areas or a failure to synthesize these relative advantages into a coherent operation exposes one to failure. In these terms, such historic upsets usually resulted from the underdog having a relative advantage in at least one of the arenas enumerated above and/or a failure of the favorite to develop and execute a concept of operations that accommodated for this particular lack of a relative advantage.

To give them the credit they deserve, both Sun Tzu (importance of knowing) and Clausewitz (fog) identified the existence of relative advantages in the information and cognitive domains. However, these ideas have yet to be regularly factored into many net assessments that compare two sides. The emphases of these assessments unfortunately remain focused on force structure. With the increasing importance of Information Superiority as a fundamental enabler of emerging operational concepts (e.g., *Joint Vision 2020*), it is hoped that more attention will be focused on the arenas identified here in the information and cognitive domains. Exactly what we mean by relative advantage is described and illustrated in the following sections, beginning with a description of the concept of a relative information advantage.

Understanding that competitive advantage is the synthesis of a number of relative advantages leads to a recognition of the importance of the development of mission capability packages that properly balance and integrate capabilities from all of the domains.

Key Capabilities for a 21st Century Military

As we prepare for an uncertain future, and as we continue to undertake the kind of missions that defined military operations in the final decade of the 20th century, we need to develop exactly the kind of qualities that (1) are enabled by improved information and communications technologies and (2) have been lacking in traditional concepts of operation, military organizations, and approaches to command and control.

We increasingly need to be highly responsive, adaptable, flexible, and precise in our application of force. The fog and friction of war may be significantly reduced but they will never go away. They will continue to be enemy number one. Learning how we can reduce them where possible and how to deal with them effectively if necessary is the fundamental challenge of Information Age Warfare.

The stakes are high, and we must find a way to balance two critical risks—the risks associated with abandoning tried-and-true methods of dealing with the fog and friction of war without thoroughly understanding the new ways of doing business and the risks associated with failing to attain the capabilities that the new ways of doing business provide. If history is a guide, we will err on the side of not embracing the new ways of doing business rapidly enough. Only time will tell what the true cost of this error will be.

Given this institutional inclination our only hope lies in trying to accelerate progress toward a better understanding and acceptance of what we can do with the incredible capabilities that the Information Age is giving to us.

What's Different?

In order to put the Information Age into focus it is necessary to identify those things that are (or soon will be) different. This section addresses technological capabilities, the economics of information and communications, emerging concepts that are designed to leverage information, and the pace of change. These are the key attributes that distinguish the Information Age from previous eras.

Information Age Technologies

Technological advances in recent years have vastly increased our capability to collect, process, disseminate, and utilize information. Airborne and space-based sensors are, for example, capable of providing real-time pictures of increasing dimensionality (hyper-spectral) and resolution. Perhaps the most significant advances have come in the technologies related to the distribution of information. Our ability to broadcast information, distribute it to a large audience, or to deliver it in a more focused manner (narrowcast), even to individuals on the go, has dramatically increased. However, despite considerable advances in our ability to process information, these advances have not been rapid enough to keep pace with the increases in collection. Humans are still required to make sense of what is collected. That will remain the case for sometime to come. However, help is on the way. Technological advances in pattern recognition, analysis tools, and visualization techniques are making it increasingly easier for humans to increase their throughput as well as their ability to extract what they need from the available data and information. We can expect continuing advances, perhaps even at accelerating rates. This, in effect, will give us sooner rather than later the ability to provide access to useful information on almost any subject, anywhere, anytime.

Of perhaps even more importance, technology is bridging distances and providing the capability for individuals to be able to interact with each other in increasingly sophisticated ways, making it easier for individuals and organizations to share information, to collaborate on tasks, and to synchronize actions or effects.

But technological advances alone do not define the Information Age. Of ultimate importance is what is being done with these newly provided technical capabilities. That is, enabling individuals and organizations to create value in new ways. Of most immediate interest to the conduct of warfare are new concepts of organization. These new organizational forms involve changes in the way authority is exercised and the way that control is maintained. In numerous instances these new organizational forms have outperformed their more traditional competitors. One of the features of these new organizational forms that is of great interest to military organizations is their increased ability to adapt to a dynamic environment. Of equal importance is the virtual nature of these organizations that gives them the ability to be assembled rapidly, to minimize travel (to move information—not people), and to compress time by being able to effectively maintain 24-hours-per-day, 7-days-per-week (24 X 7) operations.

Richness and Reach

The explosion of information and communications technologies has dramatically altered the economics of information. In *Blown to Bits*, Evans and Wurster introduced the concepts of information richness and reach to explain how the Internet has changed the economics of information.[1] They defined information richness as an aggregate measure of the quality of information and information reach as an aggregate measure of the degree that information is shared. Historically, one was forced to choose between a rich information exchange with very limited reach (e.g., face-to-face discussion aided by graphics, maps) or a restricted information exchange that had a wider reach (e.g., memos, dispatch).

This choice was forced because in the past the economics of information dictated an inverse relationship between the richness of the information that could be exchanged and the number of individuals it could be exchanged with. This inverse relationship can be described by a tradeoff as illustrated in Figure 21 showing the boundary between Industrial Age and Information Age possibilities. The key variables that influence the shape and location of this curve are the state-of-the-art information technology and its underlying economics.

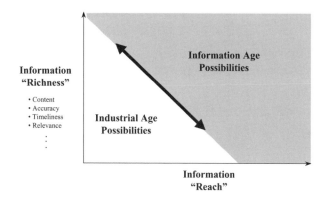

Figure 21. The Information Domain

As individuals and organizations have become better able to extend their reach, they have begun to focus on the quality of reach as well as simply the quantitative aspects of reach. The quality of interaction has therefore been added to the richness/reach construct in Figure 22. It has only been within the last decade or so that individuals and organizations have been able to provide all three—high quality information easily disseminated to those who need it in a way that facilitates the exchange. To illustrate progress in the quality of interaction, consider the nature of the exchanges in military operations that take place between and among battlespace entities. As the state of the art in information technology advanced, military communications progressed from runners to smoke signals and signal flags to telegraph to radio to telephone to video teleconferencing to a fully functioning collaborative work environment.

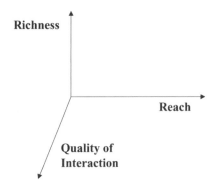

Figure 22. Richness, Reach, and Quality of Interaction

Information Age Opportunities

Being able to move into a new part of the three dimensional space depicted in Figure 22 provides military organizations with an opportunity to significantly improve the key links in the value chain that link information technology to mission effectiveness. The opportunity now exists for a military organization to make enormous gains in its ability to share information (extend reach). This is because technology now enables organizations to distribute and share information without significantly degrading its richness. Improvements in the ability to share information will contribute to improvements in the ability to generate and maintain shared awareness which in turn, together with the greatly enhanced facilities to collaborate (quality of interaction), will contribute to improved synchronization. Thus, advances in the information domain that result from an improved ability to push the envelope in the richness, reach, and interaction space will affect processes in the cognitive domain which in turn will be reflected in the physical domain in the form of responsiveness, adaptability, agility, and flexibility. These competencies will provide a source of competitive advantage in the Information Age.

Accommodating Change by Coevolution

It is not only the new capabilities and concepts that accompany the Information Age that are different, but also the nature of the technology itself and the ever increasing rate of change that make our times very different. The discomfort associated with the nature of the changes combined with the incredibly rapid pace of change and the very high cost of error associated with decisions that involve our national security create a formidable set of challenges. The usual bureaucratic reaction is paralysis. In these circumstances, however, this reaction only puts us further behind and makes it more difficult to respond to the national security challenges ahead.

Both blitzkrieg and carrier aviation can and should be viewed as disruptive innovations because over time they first threatened and then disrupted the established values and processes of their respective organizations. In the case of the German Army, it was the infantry that was threatened and disrupted. In the case of the U.S. Navy, it was the battleship admirals.

As will become clear in the sections that follow, Network Centric Warfare can and should be viewed as a disruptive innovation. Key aspects and attributes of Network Centric Warfare are fundamentally disruptive in nature. For example, information sharing and collaboration disrupt existing organizational decisionmaking processes, authorities, and values.

Allocating resources to networks threatens existing platform-centric power structures. If existing platforms and their associated tactics, techniques, and procedures were clearly decisive in *Operation Desert Shield, Desert Storm*, why should Network Centric Warfare be relevant? In the present absence of a peer competitor, the compelling rationale for pursuing disruptive innovation in the form of Network Centric Warfare may be lacking.

Since the beginning of the Information Age, commanders have been concerned about how information technologies would affect information flow on the battlefield. A look at *The Unintended Consequences of Information Age Technologies*,[2] (requested by General John Shalikashvili, a former Chairman of the Joint Chiefs of Staff) concluded that changes in the flow of information could be dysfunctional if these changes were not also accompanied by changes to concepts of operation, doctrine, organization, command concepts, training, and other elements of a mission capability package.

The solution lies in the concept of coevolution of mission capability packages. A mission capability package consists of a concept of operations and an approach to command and control, along with tailored organization, doctrine, education and training, systems, and material (including weapons and platforms).[3] [4] This concept works because it explicitly encourages and facilitates tuning all of the elements necessary to develop and deploy an operational concept designed to leverage new capabilities. Information Age technologies and the innovations they enable are disruptive because they require that key elements of a mission capability package change in order to reap the benefits that the new capability can provide. Command concepts and organizational forms have, in the past, proven to be very resistant to change, yet it is critical that they adapt if information is to be fully leveraged. Thinking about mission capability packages rather than technology insertion causes us to focus on the need for change to take place simultaneously in a number of dimensions. Coevolution dramatically reduces the time it takes to develop and field integrated solutions and allows for a continuing process that is better able to keep pace with the changes that are taking place.

---

[1]Phillip B. Evans and Thomas S. Wurster, "Strategy and the New Economics of Information," *Harvard Business Review* (September-October 1997).

[2]David S. Alberts, *The Unintended Consequences of Information Age Technologies: Avoiding the Pitfalls, Seizing the Initiative* (Washington, DC: National Defense University Press, 1996).

[3]David S. Alberts, John J. Garstka, Frederick P. Stein, "Implications for MCPs," *Network Centric Warfare: Developing and Leveraging Information Superiority*, 2nd Edition (Revised) (Washington, DC: CCRP Publication Series, 1999).

[4]INSS Strategic Forum, Number 14, January 1995, http://www.ndu.edu/inss/strforum/z1405.html

CHAPTER 4

Fundamentals of Information Superiority and Network Centric Warfare

Τhis chapter provides definitions of Information Superiority (IS) and Network Centric Warfare (NCW) to serve as a point of departure for a more detailed understanding of these concepts. These definitions are meant to provide the reader with a general sense of these concepts in preparation for a detailed discussion of each of the key concepts associated with these terms and the relationships between Information Superiority and Network Centric Warfare and between Network Centric Warfare and mission effectiveness.

Fundamentals of Information Superiority

Information Superiority is a state of imbalance in one's favor (relative advantage) in the information domain[1] that is achieved by being able to get the right information to the right people at the right time in the right form while denying an adversary the ability to do the same.[2] This way of thinking about Information Superiority combines a specific outcome associated with Information Superiority and the method that is used to achieve it.

Information Superiority derives from the ability to create a relative information advantage vis-à-vis an adversary. The concept of an information advantage is not new. Commanders have always sought—and sometimes gained—a decisive information advantage over their adversaries. Indeed surprise, one of the immutable principles of war, can be viewed as a type of information advantage that one force is able to establish over another.

Information Advantage

Some have mistakenly thought of an information advantage simply in terms of the information and communications capabilities that one force has in comparison to an adversary. This idea leads to an over emphasis on information processes—collection, analysis, dissemination, and so forth. But this is not what information advantage is all about. Rather, it is important to assess a force's information capabilities relative to their needs. Concepts of operation; command approaches; organizational forms; doctrine; tactics, techniques, procedures (TTPs); rules of engagement (ROEs); level of education and training; and the characteristics of weapons systems (taken together these all form a mission capability package) determine a force's information-related needs. The ability of a force to successfully carry out a military operation depends in large part on the degree to which its information needs are met.

Information needs can vary considerably. Throughout history military organizations, doctrine, command concepts, and tactics, techniques, procedures (TTPs) were designed to minimize the amount of information and communications required because capabilities in these areas were very limited. The information-related capabilities we currently have allow us to develop mission capability packages that can take advantage of our advanced information capabilities, but do not force our adversaries to mirror us in this regard. Therefore, there is no information gap or information arms race that we can force on an opponent. Consequently we will face adversaries whose information-related needs will be asymmetrical to ours. What will matter is which force does a better job satisfying their respective information needs, not which side has better information-related capabilities. Thus the advantage is determined by comparing each side's information capabilities relative to their needs.

Simply minimizing one's information-related needs is, however, not a winning strategy. However, matching concepts of operations to information-related capabilities is a prerequisite for success. Advantages accrue to organizations that successfully master the art of creating and leveraging an information advantage. Using Information Age technologies, organizations can put Information Age concepts to work moving information rather than people, conducting distributed operations, and substituting information for mass. The key is to find the right balance in which information-related capabilities are matched with a concept of operations, organization, approach to command and control, and the capabilities of the people and the weapons systems.

An information advantage can:

- Be persistent or it can be transitory.

- Exist in some areas of the battlespace but not others.

- Be measured in the context of a task or set of tasks.

- Be created by taking actions to reduce our information needs and /or increase the information needs of an adversary.

- Be achieved through the synergistic conduct of information operations, information assurance, and information gain and exploitation.[3]

There is historic precedence of the impact that the possession of relative information advantage can have in warfare. During World War II, a key contributor to the success of *Operation Overlord*, the Allied invasion of Europe in June of 1944, was the ability of Allied forces to establish and maintain an information advantage at the operational level of war. The ability of the Allied intelligence apparatus to break German codes and keep Allied codes secure gave Senior Allied Commanders confidence that the vast deception operation that had preceded *Operation Overlord* had succeeded.[4] Furthermore, at the time of the invasion, Allied forces were aware of the geographic positions of all but 2 of the 40-plus divisions of German Army Groups B and G.[5] [6] This significant information advantage, combined with aggressive deception operations, enabled Allied Forces to achieve surprise and a decisive force advantage on the beaches at Normandy and the surrounding countryside.[7] Nevertheless, at the tactical level, there were several instances during the invasion where Allied forces did not have an information advantage, landing craft attacked the wrong beaches, paratroopers from the 82nd and 101st Airborne Divisions were dropped (or landed) in the wrong places, and attack aircraft bombed the wrong targets.[8]

Fundamentals of Network Centric Warfare

Network Centric Warfare is warfare. To understand what is different about Network Centric Warfare one has to simultaneously focus on the three domains of warfare and the interactions among them. Network Centric Warfare involves networking in all three domains. In its fully mature form, Network Centric Warfare possesses the following characteristics:

Physical Domain:

All elements of the force are robustly networked achieving secure and seamless connectivity and interoperability.

Information Domain:

The force has the capability to share, access, and protect information to a degree that it can establish and maintain an information advantage over an adversary.

The force has the capability to collaborate in the information domain, which enables a force to improve its information position through processes of correlation, fusion, and analysis.

Cognitive Domain:

The force has the capability to develop high quality awareness and share this awareness.

The force has the capability to develop a shared understanding including commanders' intent.

The force has its capability to self-synchronize its operations.

In addition, the force must be able to conduct information operations across these domains to achieve synchronized effects in each of these domains.

The central hypothesis of Network Centric Warfare is that a force with these attributes and capabilities will be able to generate increased combat power by:

- Better synchronizing effects in the battlespace;

- Achieving greater speed of command; and

- Increasing lethality, survivability, and responsiveness.

To date, thinking about and experimenting with Network Centric Warfare concepts has tended to focus on the tactical and operational levels of warfare, but they are applicable to not only all levels of warfare but to all types of military activity from the tactical to the strategic. When network-centric concepts are applied to operations other than war, we use the term network-centric operations. At the operational level, network-centric operations provide commanders with the capability to generate precise warfighting effects at an unprecedented operational tempo, creating conditions for the rapid lockout of adversary courses of action.

Network Centric Warfare concepts dramatically improve a force's ability to quickly, efficiently, and effectively bring to bear all of its available assets to accomplish assigned missions. These improved warfighting capabilities result in part from the ability of a force to achieve a high degree of integration across a number of dimensions, the ability to substitute information for mass, and the ability to move information instead of moving people and material. Network Centric Warfare allows forces to adapt more quickly to a dynamic environment.

Network Centric Warfare Hypotheses

The fundamental characteristics of Network Centric Warfare can be described with a set of integrated hypotheses that can be systematically tested in warfighting experiments. These hypotheses can be organized into three classes.

Hypotheses of the first class deal with the relationships among *information sharing*, *improved awareness*, and *shared awareness*.

Hypotheses in the second class include those that involve the relationship between *shared awareness* and *synchronization*. For example, the effect of different degrees of *shared awareness* or *collaboration* on *synchronization*.

The third class of hypotheses involves the link between *synchronization* and *mission effectiveness*.

While at a high level of abstraction these Network Centric Warfare-related hypotheses may seem obvious—for example, that improved sharing of information will result in more shared awareness—

there are a host of specifics that need to be better understood before Network Centric Warfare concepts can be translated into real operational capabilities. For example, it is important to understand:

1. The specific conditions under which the shared information—shared awareness hypothesis is true;

2. The shape of the transfer function between information sharing and shared awareness;

3. The variables that influence this relationship (e.g., nature of the information exchange, quality of the information, degree of shared knowledge among the participants);

4. Barriers—such as information overload—that prevent shared information from becoming shared awareness; and

5. Approaches for overcoming these barriers.

Value Creation

Information Superiority and Network Centric Warfare concepts enable warfighters to create value (combat power) from information. This is nothing new. However, the information environment in which today's organizations operate is markedly different than it was just a few years ago. The richness and reach construct developed by Evans and Wurster provides a relatively straightforward approach for understanding the nature of the information environment and its relationship to the ability to create value.[9] As described in the previous chapter, this approach (at a high level of abstraction) describes the information environment as a two dimensional space with one axis being information *richness* (what we would call the quality of information) and the other axis being information *reach* (part of what we mean by information sharing). They argue that value is a function of both richness and reach.

$$\text{Value} = g\,(V_i) = f\,(\text{Richness, Reach})$$

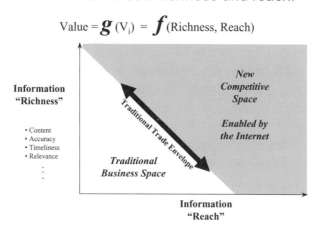

Figure 23. Value Creation

They observe that in the past information environments required tradeoffs between richness and reach (the traditional trade envelope) and that only recently have we been able to simultaneously get more of both— and by doing so are able to move to a new part of the information environment space (the part of the space in Figure 23 that is called the new competitive space).

Organizations that have learned to operate successfully in this new portion of the information environment have, in fact, been able to create an information advantage and turn it into a competitive advantage.

Value and Networks

A clear analogy can be drawn between ongoing developments in the "dot.com" space (the domain of commerce) and the emergence of Network Centric Warfare (the domain of warfare). Both seek to exploit the power of the network, which has rendered the traditional trade envelope a relic of the early phase of the Information Age. To first order, networks enable new approaches for creating value by changing the economics of information that govern the costs of reach by which a fixed level of information richness can be accessed or shared. However, in both domains, key relationships between information and value are not immediately obvious. As will be discussed later in this section, much of the trial and error that has taken place in the "dot.com" space to date has revolved around trying to figure how to create sustainable business models that leverage the new economics of information to create value.

In network-centric operations, the power of the network is manifested in the following ways, some of which do not, as yet, appear to have direct commercial analogies.

1. Increasing Richness through Increased Reach: Networks enable information richness to be increased by enabling information from multiple sources to be shared, correlated, fused, and accessed.

2. Increased Shared Awareness: Networks contribute to the generation of shared awareness by enabling richness to be shared.

3. Improved Collaboration: Networks enable information sharing which transforms shared awareness into collaborative planning and synchronized actions that create a competitive advantage.

Network Attributes

Different networks and related services can be compared using the diagram depicted in Figure 24. The circle is divided into three regions—one for richness, one for reach (including quality of interaction), and one for value. Attributes of richness, reach, and value are represented by radii.

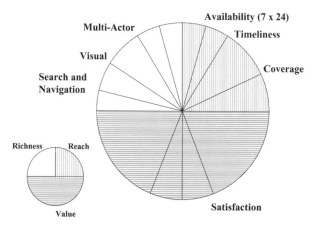

Figure 24. Network Attributes

Network Comparison

The richness and reach attributes of two networks, the voice network (the telephone system) and the Internet (which is, in fact, a value-added network riding on top of a phone-like network) are compared in Figure 25 (this type of diagram is sometimes referred to as a "Kiveat Diagram"). Note that the two richness and reach profiles do not overlap completely. One cannot say which is better or which creates more value without a specification of the attributes of value associated with a given individual or organization and with a given task to be performed or decision to be made. For many situations and tasks, the telephone system provides the right mix of richness and reach. Similarly, in other situations and tasks, the richness and reach provided by the Internet can provide increased value.

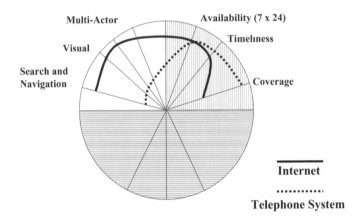

Figure 25. Network Comparison

Comparing Business Models

The information positions of Borders, a brick and mortar company, and Amazon.com, an e-business, are portrayed in Figure 26. Note that, to first order, Amazon.com achieves both greater information richness and reach. The value propositions of these two companies are compared in Figure 27. This figure portrays key relationships among richness, reach, and value. Each value proposition has dominant attributes. For example, consider a customer decision to purchase a book. If a customer wants to browse a book before purchasing (a type of richness), then bricks and mortar wins hands down. If a customer is interested in reading customer reviews of a book, then online dominates. If there is some sense of urgency associated with the purchase (e.g., an upcoming birthday party), then bricks and mortar dominates. If selection is important, then online provides a key advantage. The largest bricks and mortar bookstores stock approximately 300,000 books, while the larger online stores have a selection of over 6 million. If cost is an issue, than online may or may not have the advantage. If total time spent on the transaction (minus delivery) is important, than online dominates. When time for wrapping and mailing are factored in, then online can be even more compelling. From this analysis, it is clear that the decision that a customer makes with respect to where to purchase a book is a function of their individual preferences (weight that the customer places on specific attributes).

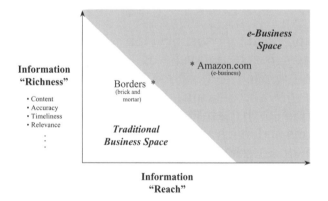

Figure 26. Commercial Example

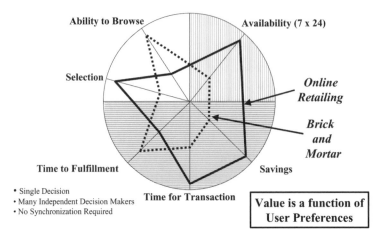

Figure 27. Comparing Business Models

Military Value Chain

The approach for describing the relationship between richness, reach, and value in the commercial sector can be applied to describe key relationships in the military value chain. Figure 28 portrays key relationships in the military value chain. In this diagram, richness and reach are used to describe an information advantage, command and control is represented with quality of interaction, and combat power is the value metric. This graphical technique enables multi-dimensional relationships between the information domain, the cognitive domain, and the physical domain to be visualized.

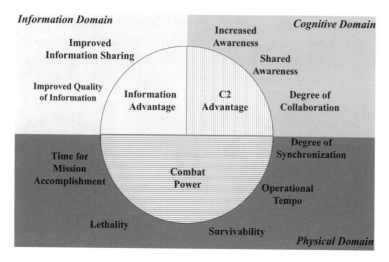

Figure 28. Military Value Chain

An advantage in the information domain can be described using the attributes of richness and reach. An advantage in the cognitive domain can be described using the attributes of increased awareness and shared awareness. Both of these attributes are important because particular innovation may only increase the quality of awareness or only share a previously achieved level of awareness. Some innovations may, in fact, affect both either positively or negatively. Command and control is, among other things, concerned with communicating the nature of the mission and circumstances with others. The degree to which members of the force can share information is related to the degree of interoperability that exists, while the manner in which they operate is related to the degree of collaboration. Figure 28 provides a number of attributes associated with combat power. These attributes are logically arranged from right to left as the degree of synchronization may be related to the operational tempo that can be achieved, which in turn may affect lethality and survivability which may be related to the time required to achieve the mission. The attributes for combat power that are selected will depend upon the situation.

Comparing Warfighting Models

An idealized network-centric warfighting model is compared with a platform-centric model in Figure 29. Because of the increased access to information that a network-centric model provides to battlespace entities, those entities can have both better information and an improved ability to generate shared awareness than a platform-centric model, which restricts the flow of information. A network-centric model can also achieve higher levels of interoperability and collaboration. As a result, the network-centric model can do a better job of synchronizing actions. This in turn makes it possible to achieve increased OPTEMPO, survivability, and lethality as well as reducing the time required for mission accomplishment. While Figure 29 is a notional view, these assertions (testable hypotheses) are fully supported by the emerging evidence which is discussed later in this volume.

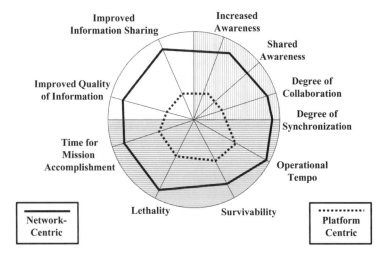

Figure 29. Comparing Warfighting Models

Figure 30 depicts an improved information position that is made possible by improvements in both richness and reach enabled by networking the force. Thus, the networked force has access to a region of the information domain that was previously unattainable.

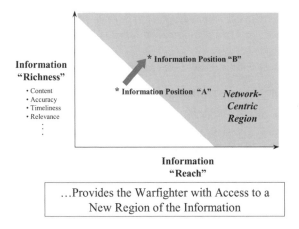

Figure 30. Networking the Force

The relative locations in the information domain determine the nature of the advantage. In this example the gains in richness and reach are presumed to be roughly proportional, though there is no reason to believe that the impact of a particular innovation will be symmetric. Many of the similar improvements (changes in communications technologies) are largely improvements in reach or the quality of interactions. Others provide greater richness. Building information advantages will often require conscious choices about the balance among these factors.

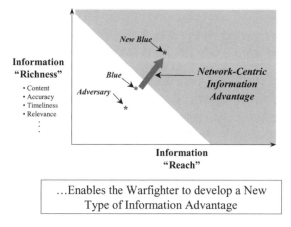

...Enables the Warfighter to develop a New Type of Information Advantage

Figure 31. Networking the Force (con.)

One key difference between the alternative warfighting models is depicted in Figure 32. The difference (represented by the upper left hand quadrant of the circle in Figure 29) is in the quality of awareness and the ability to share it—the richness and rich dimensions in the information and cognitive domain. This can only be achieved by robustly networking the force.

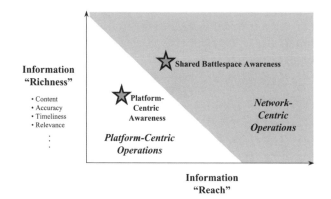

Figure 32. Platform vs. Network-Centric Awareness

New Mental Model

A network-centric concept of warfighting is not simply an improvement or extension of a platform-centric model, but involves a new way of thinking about military operations—a new mental model—as depicted in Figure 33. This new mental model is focused upon sharing and collaboration to create increased awareness, shared awareness, enabling collaboration, and, as a result, improved synchronization. This model modifies the existing linear, sequential model in which information is collected, processed, and provided to a decisionmaker for decision and then action. The new mental model serves to integrate military operations and provides an opportunity to employ new, more responsive approaches to command and control.

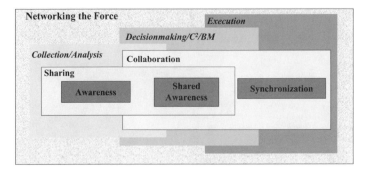

Figure 33. New Mental Model

Domain Interactions

A great deal of attention has been focused upon the semantics of information, information advantage, and Information Superiority. Until the defense community reaches a consensus on a common language, it will be increasingly burdened by the need to define terms and the promulgation of insights that are not really insights at all but are a result of differences in semantics. Figure 33, New Mental Model, utilizes terms from different domains. That is because it is designed to make the point that, in the final analysis, military operations are about trying to achieve effects in cognitive domain of an adversary (e.g., surrender, cease hostilities). To achieve this, synchronization must take place in the physical domain (potentially in the information domain as well, in the case of information operations) to create effects in the battlespace. In order to achieve this, we must first achieve effects in the cognitive domain. The new mental model captures the interactions among each of the domains—the information, the cognitive, and the physical (Figure 34). Figures 35, 36, and 37 further illustrate these views. The views differ in regard to the nature of what is being shared, the nature of collaboration, and the object of synchronization.

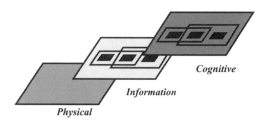

Figure 34. Domain Interactions

Information Elements

To understand the new mental model one needs to start with the view from the information domain (Figure 35) with the sharing of information and with collaboration designed to help ensure quality information (e.g., identify and resolve conflicting information). The result is what we would call a common operational picture—that is with a synchronized set of information across the battlespace.

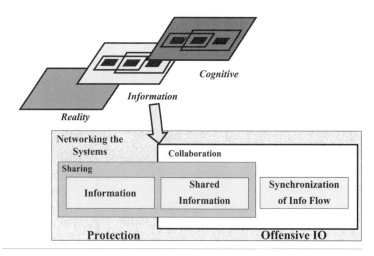

Figure 35. Information Elements

Cognitive Elements

The next step in understanding the new mental model is to move to the view from the cognitive domain (Figure 36). It is here that the distinction between information and awareness is made. From this perspective, it is awareness and shared awareness that are increased by sharing and collaboration with decisions (across the battlespace) being the object of effects to synchronize.

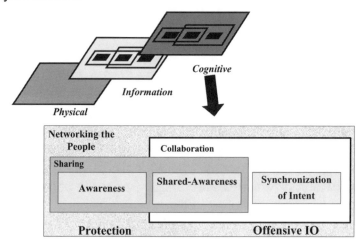

Figure 36. Cognitive Elements

Physical Elements

In the physical domain view (Figure 37), it is resources that are being shared, actions that are the object of collaboration, and battlefield effects that are being synchronized.

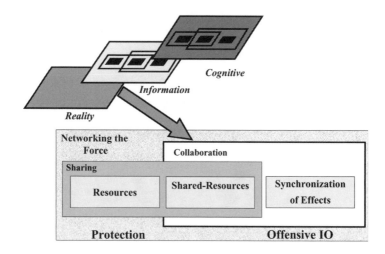

Figure 37. Physical Elements

Network Centric Warfare Value Chain

Thus, the new mental model is really a synthesis of what needs to occur in each of the domains. Figure 38 depicts the relation between the results of sharing and collaboration integrated across the domains and our goal of achieving a competitive advantage. Working back from this desired result, a competitive advantage derives from achieving both decision superiority and the ability to execute.

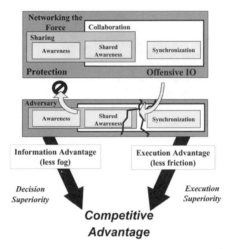

Figure 38. Network Centric Warfare Value Chain

Decision superiority is enabled by an information advantage, which can be thought of as having less fog compared to an adversary, and execution superiority enabled by less friction.

Key elements of the Network Centric Warfare value chain and their relationship are portrayed in Figure 39. This figure highlights the links in the value chain as they relate to key Information Superiority and Network Centric Warfare concepts and also places these concepts in the appropriate domain.

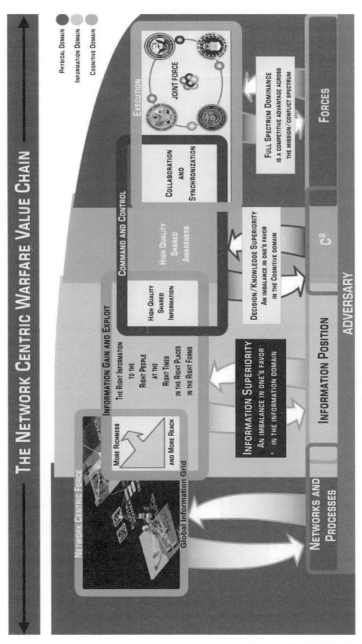

Figure 39. Value Chain Links of Information Superiority and Network Centric Warfare

Thus the new mental model can be described with a set of linkage hypotheses, each of which deals with a specific link in the value chain. While each of these linkage hypotheses may seem reasonable or even tautological to some, they need to be explicitly tested to understand the nature of the relationships between and among the links in the value chain and the conditions under which these relationships exist. Equally important, efforts to gather empirical evidence about these hypothesis and the circumstances where they apply will provide important evidence about how they can be realized. It should be noted that these hypotheses are both within and across domains, with the domain providing a clue as to where and what to instrument.

Information Quality

The information domain serves both as the linkage between reality and the cognitive domain (inside people's heads) and as the medium by which information (technically data, information, pre-real time knowledge, images, and understandings about the current and projected situation) is stored, retrieved, and disseminated. The information domain can be interpersonal (voice, face to face) or manifested in machines, such as computers and communications systems.

The discussion that follows first addresses the concept of information quality and how it has been measured in the past. These basic measures and attributes remain relevant in the information age, although they can and should be organized and understood in some new ways to better reflect current thinking and future applications. The information domain's major dimensions are then explored: information richness, information reach, and the quality of interactions in the information domain. Finally, the difficult topic of measuring information advantage is addressed in some detail.

Linkage Models and Indicants of Information Value

A classic description of how information has been valued successfully was taken from work done two decades ago.[10] This approach recognizes a distinction between the attributes of the information itself and the systems that supply, store, retrieve, and disseminate information. It also notes that information quality impacts a variety of decision variables, within the C4ISR system, that do not, themselves, represent value to the military organization. Rather these intermediate decision variables enrich the C4ISR process and improve the likelihood of effective force performance. This intermediate level of measures of system performance is expected to correlate with better decisions because the higher quality processes (faster decisions of equivalent quality, greater variety of futures considered, more options generated and evaluated, etc.) have been shown (in small group research, research into decisionmaking under stress, and some studies of military decisionmaking) to correlate with better (more effective) decisions. While these intermediate measures occur and must be measured in the cognitive domain, their impact (the true value of information) is in the reality, or physical, domain and must be measured there.

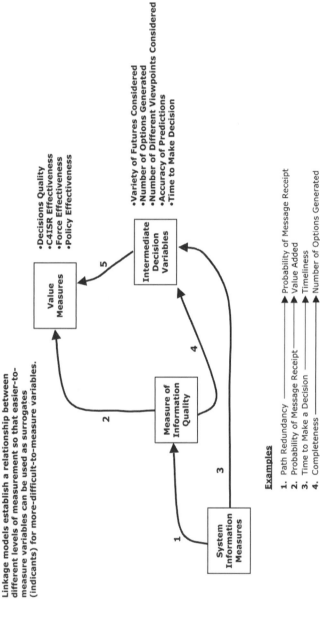

Figure 40. Linkage Models and Indicants of Information Value

This same figure also illustrates some of the more straightforward linkages among these sets. For example, one way an information system is seen as better is through path redundancy. This attribute is a major advantage of network-centric systems. Given that greater redundancy, the likelihood that any given message will be received goes up, making the typical currency and completeness of information higher for all command centers and actors that are connected to the system. This, in turn, increases both the quality of awareness of the actors in the field and that of the intermediate decisionmakers, and the degree of shared awareness among them. Note, however, that these processes are not automatic. The quality of the information itself and of the information systems must be augmented by appropriate doctrine, training, organization, leadership, and education in order to improve mission effectiveness in any given mission context.

Direct measurement of value added is impossible. Good command arrangements can, however, be recognized by a variety of indicants, or measures, that reflect good process but are not success in and of themselves. For example, good decisionmaking is associated with:

- Reflecting the uncertainty inherent in situations that consider multiple possible futures;

- Keeping the number of alternatives considered (futures assessed and courses of action considered) within the cognitive limits of most participants—3 to 7 alternatives at most;

• Gathering information from, and involving in decisionmaking councils, all the actors who are relevant; and

• Looking ahead at potential counter-measures from opponents of any particular course of action, including coalition partners.

In essence, these types of measures are defenses against failure to consider complex interactions or unintended consequences and other errors that creep into complex decisionmaking systems.[11]

Measuring Information Quality

Measuring the quality of information actually requires dealing with three interrelated issues:

• How good are the individual items in the information system (i.e., the specific items of data and information that are present);

• How good is the security of the information system being used; and

• How good is the underlying information system with respect to features not directly related to security.

Note, also, that information quality and the qualities of the supporting information systems are never, in and of themselves, going to impact effectiveness (mission accomplishment, force effectiveness, etc.). Rather information and information system qualities are always measures of performance. In other words, better information is never an end in itself. Therefore, measures of information performance must be related to measures of effectiveness such as command and control, force, and policy effectiveness.

However, better information is explicitly hypothesized to improve important components in other domains:

- Situation Awareness (SA) in the cognitive arena;

- Decisionmaking (DM) in the cognitive domain;

- Planning (including collaboration planning) in the cognitive domain; and

- Synchronization of actions in the reality domain.

Hence, better information and better information systems are expected to improve effectiveness *indirectly*, and those impacts should be measured when such research is possible. This permits diagnostic analysis of whether the better information and information systems are associated with better success.

Quality of Information Items

Research reaching back to the early 1980s has converged on a relatively simple set of measures for assessing the quality of the information available about a situation. This work originated with the HEAT (Headquarters Effectiveness Assessment Tool) program begun by DISA (then DCA) and the Joint Directors of Laboratories and was extended into the ACCES (Army Command and Control Evaluation System) research sponsored by the Army Research Institute. The approach has proven robust, supporting applications to real world crises and combat situations in historical reconstructions, exercises, and experiments more than 50 times, covering more than 150 command centers. Applications have included Joint Task Forces, US Army Corps, Divisions, and Brigades, Naval Fleets and Battle Groups, as well as non-military decisionmaking by Department of State Task Forces and corporate crisis management.

The five crucial dimensions for measuring the quality of information available within a command center are:

- Completeness (are all the relevant items available, including entities, their attributes, and relationships between them);

- Correctness (are all the items in the system faithful representations of the realities they describe);

- Currency (age of the items of information, often termed their latency);

- Accuracy or Level of Precision (which is conditional on the purpose the user has in mind); and

- Consistency across different command centers, functionally specialized arenas, and applications.

These five attributes are independent. Information can be complete but incorrect, current but inconsistent, inaccurate but complete, and so forth. Indeed, trade-offs between these five attributes are commonplace. For example, research in the HEAT and ACCES programs showed that efforts to make data more complete were often associated with lower correctness.

All of these attributes may, at times, be conditioned on the needs of a particular mission or aspect of the battlespace. For example, tolerable latency may be seconds (missile defense), minutes (outer air battle), hours (logistics close to the front), days (theater logistics), or weeks (mobilization). Commands often establish standards for latency depending on the physical limits on information capture and processing, the physics of the mission area, their organizational capacity, and other factors. When that occurs, the metrics may be wisely designed to reflect those command standards. However, since these may be the results of doctrine or experience that does not reflect the capacity of modern information systems, assessors of information quality should normally plan on capturing and reporting detailed data (e.g., latency) as well as information about the degree to which command standards were met or violated.

Timeliness is another factor that depends on the situation. It reflects the relationship between the age of an information item and the tasks or missions it must support. In simple, physics dominated cases, timeliness requirements can be calculated. For example, the lead time necessary to knock down an incoming missile can be postulated, as can the time needed to place fire on an artillery battery that is still firing before it can move. In many cases, however, fixed timeliness requirements are incalculable because the problem is dominated by adversary decisions. For example, an infantry operation may have a limited window of opportunity for moving onto key terrain before it is occupied by the enemy. However, the length on the window is determined in part by the adversary. Does he recognize the crucial nature of the terrain? What type of force (if any) is he sending to occupy it? By what route? In what strength? Is there some other maneuver or action that either side can take that will reduce the importance of occupying this ground? Thus, if and when key terrain is occupied is both a function of the physics of a situation as well as cognitive factors that may be influenced by doctrine, training, and offensive information operations.

Hence, reliance on timeliness as a fundamental attribute of information places a major burden on the analyst to demonstrate that the target value (when is the information timely?) has been established in a valid and reliable way.

Security of Information (Information Assurance)

Regardless of the quality of information available within an information system, the assurance characteristics of the system remain a crucial concern. Decisionmakers acting on false or corrupt information are expected (hypothesized) to make worse decisions than those working on valid and reliable information (even if there are only a small number of information items which are false). Some HEAT and ACCES research has shown that even a small amount of wrong information can have a major impact on the quality of situational understanding and lower the chances of high-quality military decisions. Perhaps equally important, users must be able to trust the data and information in the systems supporting them and have confidence in the system's ability to provide them with needed information. Users who do not trust the quality of information available or do not have confidence in their information systems are believed (hypothesized) to both act more cautiously (create and select actions sets that are risk averse in that they will work even if the available information is incorrect, late, inconsistent, etc.) and more slowly (waiting for confirmatory evidence before they act on emerging patterns, deliberate longer, etc.).

In general, there are five fundamental dimensions of information assurance viewed from the perspective of the information system itself: privacy, availability, integrity, authenticity, and nonrepudiation. Taken together, these attributes describe a system that users can trust.

Privacy means just that—no one except authorized users has access and each user's access is appropriate for their roles and responsibilities. In the ideal system, no one except authorized users has any opportunity to get into the system. When that cannot be avoided (e.g., long haul communications are required), the system itself must be designed to keep out unauthorized users and to detect, with a high degree of confidence, efforts to penetrate the system.

Availability means that all the authorized users have access all of the time. This is necessary if current information is to be shared and if the user community is to develop trust and confidence in using the information in the system. An unreliable system (one that goes down or has links in it that tend to fail) both reduces user willingness to use it and also offers outsiders more opportunities for penetration. A highly reliable system, on the other hand, permits users to place trust in it and to plan on using its features, whether they are databases, images, information flows, or knowledge representations. Clearly graceful degradation is preferable to system collapse and both mean time between failures (from the user perspective) and mean time to repair are important characteristics.

Integrity is the coherence of the system and its contents. Where privacy focuses attention on whether unauthorized actors have access to the system, integrity deals with whether outsiders have the ability to tamper with the contents—deleting records, introducing false information or data, and so forth. The ideal system is tamper proof, but also monitors for efforts at tampering and contains countermeasures to prevent meddling.

Authenticity refers to the degree to which the data, information, and knowledge in the system are valid and reliable representations of what was supplied by the authorized users. Information systems are designed to accept inputs from a variety of sources. In many cases, there are authoritative actors (workstations or roles within the system) that are responsible for the quality and currency of those inputs. They are authentic when they have come from those authorized actors and not from others. Note that this does not deal with the quality of the information (it may still be incomplete, incorrect, old, etc.) but only with the appropriateness of its source(s).

Nonrepudiation is a simple characteristic. It means that each item in the information system can be traced back to its origin, through an assigned pedigree or some other technical means. Nonrepudiation is important to information assurance because it provides the road map by which users gain confidence in their data. If an insider were to be corrupted and seek to tamper with information in the system that was outside that actor's area of authority, they would want to be able to disguise or repudiate those actions within the system. Similarly, if an outsider penetrates the system and misuses a work station to tamper with items beyond the purview of that work station, the inability to repudiate the action within the system would allow information operations personnel to trace the damage back to the guilty work station. In essence, this feature prevents hiding your trail.

Measuring the security of an information system has become both a major challenge and also an arena where a great deal more work is needed. Many exercises are conducted without attacks on the information system, often because those organizing and directing the exercises are focused on training goals that would be poorly served if the information systems were compromised or taken down. Reluctance to reveal what is known about likely types of attacks is also a factor restricting exercise applications. Information systems are often tested in an *ad hoc* fashion, with a creative group of knowledgeable people given free reign to attack the system within selected time frames. Systematic reviews of all the information assurance dimensions are rare and need to become more common.

Other Desirable Qualities of Information Systems

Information systems also have a variety of attributes that, while they are not closely related to either the quality of the information in them or information assurance, make them more desirable. These other qualities can and should be measured.

Ease of use is an important quality of an information system. Its human factors should have been crafted so that its use is intuitive. This was the quality that first made "point-and-click" technologies successful. *Ease of use* can be measured in terms of the training time required to achieve some measurable level of proficiency. It can also be measured in terms of the time a trained or experienced operator requires to perform specific functions. This can be compared with baseline performance without the system. *Ease of use* is also related to the percent of the capabilities of the system that are actually used. In the case where users only take advantage of a small percentage of a system's capabilities, the investment in its other features has clearly been wasted.

Systems that are easy to use will also help users combat stress and fatigue. Command and control systems will often be used in sustained crisis action or warfare arenas. Hence, human lives will be at stake and the operators under considerable stress, perhaps even direct threat of attack. Those same operators will also be working long hours, whether the mission is humanitarian assistance, peace operations, or war. Better systems will prove their ease of use under these difficult conditions.

Differences in the cultures of users will also test a system's ease of use. U.S. doctrine for the new century anticipates coalition operations in the vast majority of military missions. Perhaps equally challenging, military personnel can anticipate working alongside civil authorities (both U.S. and foreign), non-governmental organization personnel, and international organization officials. These people often have organizational cultures very different from the military. Hence, systems that can be used by very different people, with little common background and training, are more desirable.

Command and control systems also need to be *robust*. They need to work in a wide variety of environments (physical, cultural, and threat environments), for a wide variety of purposes. In many ways, this robustness is well served by redundancy. The old, stovepipe systems are giving way to networks in part because of the inherent redundancy (and therefore robustness) of networks. Redundancy also helps to ensure that the information system degrades gracefully when it is under attack or experiences problems.

The most desirable information systems also fuse, correlate, and aggregate data or information from multiple sources to make it more useful to humans and *facilitate integrated operations*. This certainly means that they facilitate sharing data items, databases, images, information, and existing knowledge. At the same time, they must also enable collaboration over space, time, function, and echelon. All collaboration, except face-to-face, passes through the information domain. Hence, the ideal system makes that process faster and better.

The *credibility* of the system is also important. While dependent on information assurance properties, the systems credibility is, in fact, a perception. It must, therefore be measured by interviewing or surveying users. The ideal system engenders considerable trust in users—they believe it will support them effectively.

Finally, the *speed* of an information system is significant in many command and control applications. Delay in moving data, images, or information means higher risk. Adversary activities that are not known immediately to a commander can be dangerous to the force and to mission accomplishment. Delay also forces decisionmakers into selecting less risky options. Delay translates into greater uncertainty at the time decisions must be made, which generally means that the commander must hedge his decisions and not take the risk of acting precipitously. An emphasis on the speed of the information system is one of the consequences of the Information Age.

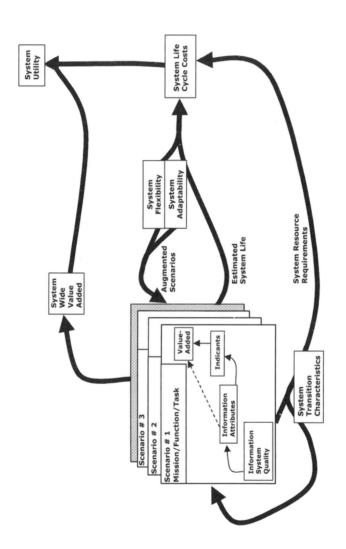

Figure 41. Determination of System's Utility

Determination of System's Utility

Bringing all these elements (richness, reach, and quality of interaction) together to provide an assessment of information system utility also requires contexts. As Figure 41 indicates, the range of operational environments where a given information domain capacity is expected to perform must be sampled (Scenarios 1...n) at the levels of mission, function, and task. Too narrow a frame for assessment will result in serious suboptimization. Given the potential for changes in the mission arena, a premium will ultimately be placed on system flexibility, adaptability, and the resultant life cycle costs. Many military systems have been reborn because they could be changed as missions and operating environments evolved. These analyses are by and large the province of budgetary specialists, but the basic information about information quality, richness, reach, and quality of interaction are essential to their efforts.

---

[1]*Joint Vision 2020*, Chairman of the Joint Chiefs of Staff, Director for Strategic Plans and Policy, J5, Strategy Division (Washington, DC: U.S. Government Printing Office, June 2000).

[2]*Information Superiority: Making the Joint Vision Happen*, Office of the Assistant Secretary of Defense (Command, Control, Communications, & Intelligence) (Washington, DC: Pentagon, November, 2000).

[3]*Ibid.*

[4]Anthony Cave Brown, *Body Guard of Lies* (New York, NY: Bantam Books, 1976), pp. 1-10, 647-687.

[5]*Ibid.*, p. 664.

[6]John Keegan, *Six Armies in Normandy: From D-Day to the Liberation of Paris* (New York, NY: Penguin Books, 1982), pp. 335-340.

[7]Anthony Cave Brown, *Body Guard of Lies* (New York, NY: Bantam Books, 1976), pp. 647-687.

[8]John Keegan, *Six Armies in Normandy: From D-Day to the Liberation of Paris* (New York, NY: Penguin Books, 1982), pp. 69-114, 131-132.

[9]Phillip B. Evan and Thomas S. Wurster, "Strategy and the New Economics of Information," *Harvard Business Review* (September-October 1997).

[10]David S. Alberts, "C2I Assessment: A Proposed Methodology," *Proceedings for Quantitative Assessment of the Utility of Command and Control System* (McLean, VA: MITRE Corporation, 1980), pp. 67-91.

[11]Irving L. Janis, *Groupthink: Psychological Studies of Decisions and Fiascoes* (Boston: Houghton Mifflin, 1982).

CHAPTER 5

Information Domain

Focus of the Discussion

The key attributes of the information domain can be subdivided into three major dimensions or vectors: the richness or quality of the information domain, the reach or distribution of the information domain, and the quality of interaction within the information domain. Each of these is, of course, multidimensional in its own right.

Attributes of Information Richness

The richness, or quality, of information has eight attributes that measure important elements of information richness and are displayed on a kiveat diagram. As discussed earlier, the attributes of information quality that have been in use for decades comprise the majority of those included in Figure 42, specifically:[1]

- Information completeness,

- Information correctness,

- Information currency,

- Information accuracy or precision, and

• Information consistency.

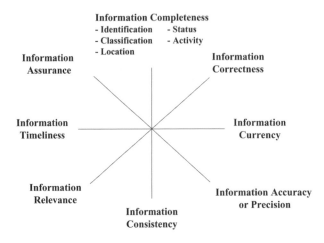

Figure 42. Information Domain: Attributes of Information Richness

However, three new attributes are also present, having been deduced from characteristics of the situation. These are, therefore, both conditional (dependent on the type of situation and actions) as well as dynamic (change over time). These three attributes are *relevance, timeliness,* and *information assurance.* They are seen as crucial additions as we move to the Information Age.

Commanders and staffs do not have the time or energy to pay attention to everything in their operating arenas. Hence, they exercise strong filters that enable them to focus on that information necessary for success. *Relevance* is a dynamic attribute, which makes it challenging to measure. However, it must be understood as a crucial element defining the information needs (richness required) to be satisfied by C4ISR systems. There is no correct or absolute answer to what constitutes relevant information—it varies across situations and times. Information Age systems must be designed to (a) provide commanders with what doctrine and their experience suggest is relevant, (b) identify changes in their information needs rapidly, and (c) allow them to acquire new information easily and promptly by shifting perspective, drilling down, or conducting rapid, intuitive searches. Errors in deciding what is relevant and systems that make it difficult for key staff and commanders to shift their perspectives or drill down when necessary are often associated with difficulties in being able to quickly understand a situation and with problems in decisionmaking.

Information *timeliness* has also been derived from the needs of commanders and key staff. While military practitioners generally agree that more recent information is preferable, they also have long recognized that the value of information often depends on its availability with respect to some military threat or opportunity. Theater ballistic missile defense depends on fractions of seconds, air defense often on seconds, tank and other direct fire battles require shooting solutions in seconds, and maneuver information in minutes. At the opposite end of the scale, theater command typically deals with days and major theater logistics in weeks.

Information *assurance* is recognized as necessary to generate user trust and confidence in the information. Hence, surveys and other instruments designed to assess user attitudes toward the information and information systems are an important element of this dimension. As discussed in the previous chapter, information assurance has a number of components, including: privacy, integrity, authenticity, availability, and nonrepudiation.

Information *completeness* has been broken down in this figure to show some of its key attributes. The most basic element is the identification of relevant entities and sets. A commander who is unaware of key parts of the enemy force, or key weather and terrain, is at peril. The correct classification of what has been observed and its correct location (both in general and in relation to other entities and sets) is also critical. Finally, the correct status (general as in strength and current mission or specific as in food, fuel, morale, water, or ammunition) and activity (attacking, digging in, rearming, etc.) often provide important insights into the military situation.

Attributes of Information Reach

Reach, or distribution, deals with the number and variety of people, work stations, or organizations that can share information. These vary across a somewhat surprising set of dimensions in the information domain, many of which are impacted directly by the increased capacity of modern information systems:

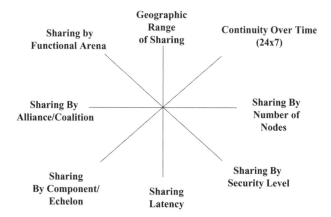

Figure 43. Information Domain: Attributes of Information Reach

- Geographic range: satellite and other long-haul systems cover more of the globe than their predecessors;

- Continuity over time: fewer gaps in coverage and mechanical failures than previous systems;

- More nodes active or available at the same time;

- More sharing at different levels of security;

- Less latency—sharing information sooner, often by having it routed automatically to a variety of users rather than a central processing location before distribution;

- More sharing across military components and echelons;

- Sharing across broader alliance and coalition organizations; and

- Sharing across more functional arenas.

Note that what occurs in the information domain is *sharing*, not collaboration. Sharing means providing data, information, images, knowledge, or understandings to another actor. *Collaboration*, on the other hand, involves active engagement by two or more parties toward a common purpose. (More about this in the Collaboration chapter). Hence, when data, reports, orders, or other items are provided to different actors, information sharing has occurred. The massive improvements in information dissemination made possible by Information Age systems are the most typical way that information reach changes. Changes in reach occur either when new technologies make something new possible or when the economics of information management or distribution changes.

Quality of Interaction

In addition to the quality or richness of information content and its reach is the nature of the interaction among actors. In the 18th century, the British Admiralty was able to control fleets around the world, but their mechanisms for interaction were extremely limited: meetings with commanders before they deployed, written orders (usually at the mission level), reports from the fleet dispatched by fast sloops, orders returned the same way, and senior officers sent out to convey instructions.

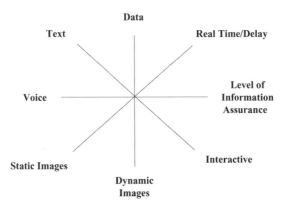

Figure 44. Information Domain: Quality of Interaction

Today, the quality of information sharing can be almost unlimited if we make the necessary investments in C4ISR. The nature of information exchanges varies considerably. Each of the following is a way of exchanging information:

• Data exchange,

• Text exchange,

• Voice,

• Static images,

• Dynamic images,

• Degree to which exchanges are interactive or reciprocal,

• Level of information assurance about the exchanges, and

• Whether the exchange is real time or delayed (by how much).

Some of these dimensions focus on sharing information, others either support or require genuine collaboration—working together toward a common purpose.

C4ISR systems have suffered from a variety of limits that are no longer technically necessary. Rather than having to choose between voice and data or dynamic images and secure images, particularly at the tactical level in the field, the bandwidth and computing power now exists to allow high quality interactions. However, they must be designed and implemented along with the key elements of organization, doctrine, training, maintenance capability, and other elements that make them both cost effective and useful in the field.

Application of Metrics: Attributes for a Single Integrated Air Picture (SIAP)

The attributes of information richness, reach, and quality of interaction have been applied to characterize the Single Integrated Air Picture (SIAP).[2] The SIAP is an instantiation of a construct in the information domain. Such constructs are developed in order to satisfy demands for mission-related information. The SIAP is focusing upon improving the following five attributes of information quality:

- *Completeness*—The percentage of real tracks that are included in the SIAP.

- *Correctness*—Data accurately reflects true track attributes (position, kinematics, and identity).

- *Commonality*—Track attributes of shared data are the same for each SIAP user.

- *Continuity*—Proper maintenance of track attributes over time.

- *Timeliness*—Data is where it is needed, when it is needed.

However, these constructs are broken down into dozens of very specific measures that reflect the information requirements of the users of the SIAP. Timeliness, for example, is broken into elements that reflect information dissolution in the context of specific applications. This type of detailed work is essential if meaningful research designs, simulations, and models are to be built and applied.

Information Needs

An information need is defined as the measurable set of information (and its quality, reach, and interaction characteristics) required to plan and/or execute a mission or task. Clearly this can cover a wide range of different items and sets of information. The information necessary to plan a theater level campaign is broad and general, with stress on the combat environment (physical features, weather, order of battle, political, social, and economic factors). The information required to strike a set of fixed targets with precision munitions needs to be quite accurate, while the information required to strike mobile targets needs to be both accurate and current.

Information Situation is measured relative to
Information Needs

Example: Positive Information Situation

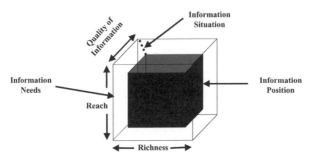

Figure 45. Information Domain: Key Relationships

The minimal information needed is defined as that set required to accomplish the task at hand, which includes achieving the level of effectiveness specified in the mission statement. This may also require efficiency metrics that reflect limits on the resources to be used in achieving that level of effectiveness.

SCUD missiles, for example, have relatively simple information needs. They might be targeted on the capital city of an adversary. Hence, the grid location for the center of mass of the enemy's capital is adequate to meet their needs. However, a commander on the other side, asked to conduct theater missile defense, has a very different set of needs. This commander needs to know (a) the locations of launchers, (b) storage locations for missiles and launchers, (c) possible movement routes, (d) firing positions, and (e) in the extreme case, precise flight path information so that incoming missiles can be targeted.

Information needs must be expressed in terms of the richness, reach, and quality of interaction required. Targeting precision guided munitions, for example, requires location accuracy down to a few meters. The information must be current if the target is mobile or if its use can change from military to civilian. Hence, there are minimum needs for richness. Reach is required to deliver the information to the target planners and the shooters. Interaction is needed to keep the information up to date, particularly when the target has dynamic features. Late updates on target location or character (e.g., from police station to location where hostages are held) can be crucial to mission success.

At a somewhat higher level focus, a commander developing a course of action wants a rich description of the operating environment, including the disposition of all forces as well as the terrain, weather, and other factors shaping the battlespace. This same set of basic information should be available to commanders at all levels and across all parts of the battlefield with no time delay (information reach), although they may require different levels of detail given their functional and geographic responsibilities. Having this set of information available helps ensure that the information is consistent across the battlespace. Finally, the ability of commanders and key staff, wherever they are located, to ask questions about battlespace information, point out apparent anomalies, and offer updates is also crucial.

In non-traditional missions the range of information that must be available to the commander and staff extends across political, military, economic, social, and information (media, etc.) arenas. Failure to recognize the full range of these information needs can create serious problems. For example, failure to understand the importance of clan structures proved costly to U.S. and UN operations in Somalia.

Information Position and Situation

The *Information Position* of an actor is defined as its information state (an aggregate of its richness, reach, and the quality of interaction) at a given point in time. In essence, this is a summary of how much information the actor possesses.

The *Information Situation* of an actor, by contrast, reflects the difference between an actor's information position and the information needs of the situation. This difference between them can be calculated if the needs and position are measured in the same way. However, this calculation may prove cumbersome unless some simplifying system (assumptions, multi-attribute utility values, or other explicit system to integrating the key dimensions and attributes) is applied.

Key Relationships

The relationships between information needs, information position, and information situation are depicted in Figure 45. The three conceptual dimensions underlying these graphics correspond with information richness, reach, and quality of interaction. The shape itself, a cube, is unrealistic, both in that these three values would not necessarily be equal (though needs could be normalized to make them equivalent) and the information position would almost never be fully symmetric.

In the example shown, the actor has a negative information position—the information available is less than the minimum required. This concept has considerable power, despite the practical issues inherent in operationalizing it. However, it does not provide any meaningful insight into the value of extra information. The information situation can be described in terms of the volumetric difference between needs and position. Because of the definition of information needs, a force that does not achieve that level can be expected to have problems accomplishing its mission. However, the implications of a positive information position are not theoretically obvious. That a force could gain a great deal of advantage from this excess information may be obvious, but there is no way to estimate its value without establishing a link between information needs and performance.

Given this formulation, a superior information position is achieved by undertaking three types of actions:

- Enhancing collection, processing, information management, and dissemination of needed information;

- Providing information assurance to protect those activities; and

- Acting to degrade the adversary's information position through offensive information operations.

Maintaining and enhancing one's own information position is a dynamic, two-sided effort in most real-world situations because adversaries are always seeking to deny crucial information or damage our information position. Achieving Information Superiority means seeking to maximize the difference between information positions, thereby maximizing the information advantage of friendly forces.

Relative Information Advantage

As illustrated in Figure 46, *relative information advantage* must be conceptualized and measured in terms of the different forces' information positions, not their information situations. In the case shown, Blue has a much greater information need, but has nevertheless come closer to fulfilling those needs than his adversary. While both forces are in a negative information position, the Red force has been much less successful relative to its own requirements. Hence, Blue would be seen as having a relative information advantage.

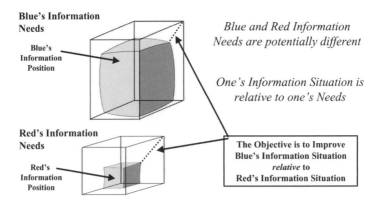

Figure 46. Relative Information Advantage

Impact of Information Operations

Information Age Warfare will place a premium on information operations. Both sides will seek to employ a range of tools to ensure achieving and maintaining an information advantage. These will include classic military techniques, such as destruction of assets or information denial and deception; technical approaches, such as jamming and interception; computer techniques, such as viruses and Trojan horses; as well as the use of public communications media. Information operations also include exploitation of the information systems of the adversary or items taken from it. The goal, however, remains the same—creation of a decisive information advantage.

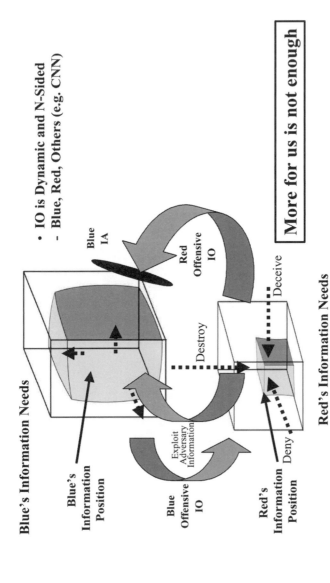

Figure 47. Impact of Information Operations

Symmetric/Asymmetric Information Needs

As illustrated by Figure 48, symmetric information needs occur when the forces of two or more competitors have equivalent requirements. This generally implies that they have similar force structures, doctrines, and levels of training. By way of contrast, asymmetric information needs arise when one force requires more information to achieve its missions than the other.

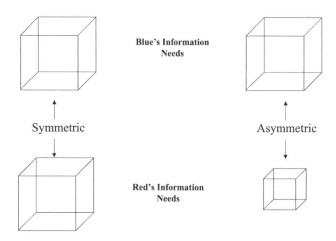

Figure 48. Information Needs

Hence, more modern forces (and the United States will typically field the more modern force in most situations) will often have a greater information need than their adversaries. These needs extend not only to the richness, reach, and interaction quality needed in the information domain, but also to protecting the information system and its contents. At the same time, the more modern force should also have some advantage in terms of its abilities to collect and process data and information, and to attack the adversary's information systems and their contents. This may be the crucial difference when two forces have very different information needs.

Determinants of Information Needs

A number of factors influence the level of information need for a given force and hence the likelihood that an asymmetric situation will occur. These include, but are not limited to:

• Offensive or defensive orientation,

• Differing doctrines,

• Differing concepts of operation,

• Different types of weapons and platforms,

• Willingness to accept risk,

• Willingness to accept casualties and losses of equipment, and

• Differing levels of desire to minimize collateral damage.

Here, again, the United States, as the more modern force with the greatest desire to avoid casualties and collateral damage, and relying on platforms and weapons that are based on leading edge information systems, will almost always find itself with the larger need for information.

Examples

The classic examples of symmetric information operations occur across air, land, and sea warfare. In an air-to-air battle, two forces with modern platforms and C4ISR systems share the same information needs—their needs are symmetric. They are interested in the locations of each other's aircraft and other assets in the fight. Similarly, a tank battle between modern forces provides a symmetric demand for information—where are the enemy forces, what are they doing, etc. Naval battles, largely conducted with aircraft and missiles, share this symmetric information structure.

Guerrilla warfare, particularly when it uses terrorism as a tactic, on the other hand, is the classic case of asymmetric information needs. The insurgent forces require relatively little information, and most of what they need is not time sensitive. They can plant bombs, lay mines, and set ambushes without knowing when they will actually launch attacks and often without concern about collateral damage. Conventional forces fighting them, however, need quite precise information in order to locate and defeat them. Even more information is needed if collateral damage, which often alienates the general population, is to be avoided. As the Russians have learned in both Afghanistan and Chechnya, and the Americans learned in Vietnam, this information can be exceptionally difficult to obtain and keep up to date. In these situations, the more conventional force often finds it advantageous to adapt its tactics in order to reduce its dependence on information. For example, small unit operations that depend upon local/organic information capabilities have proven effective in many guerrilla conflicts, such as in Malaysia and the Philippines.

Estimating Information Advantage

As noted earlier, finding meaningful metrics and ways of making them comparable for any of the key elements of information advantage (information needs, information situation, or information position), or reliable and valid ways to compare them and interpret the results, will be a challenge.

The symmetric case is probably somewhat easier. Here the two forces' needs are assumed to be approximately the same, so estimating relative information position requires only a valid and reliable approach to estimating each side's information situation. The three key drivers are the same as for estimating needs—richness, reach, and quality of interaction—although the effectiveness of each side's offensive information operations may be a complicating factor. Even in this situation, however, interpretation of the results will require careful thought. Either side in a negative information position must, by definition, be assumed to have great difficulty achieving its mission. On the other hand, if both forces are in a positive information position, they are seen as having adequate information to achieve their mission. Even if one has a considerably greater information position, and therefore a relative advantage, the other cannot be assumed to fail since it has at least adequate information to achieve its own mission.

The same factors make operationalizing relative information advantage even more difficult when the information needs are asymmetric. However, this case is worse since positive information positions are very difficult to compare. In essence, this problem arises from the fact that once the threshold value of adequate information necessary to achieve the mission is reached, there is no readily available standard by which additional information can be valued. The obvious quantitative answer, express the gain as a percentage of the information need, has no logical relationship to likelihood of mission success except to simply say the likelihood has increased. Hence, these values cannot be compared across cases. Only in the very narrow knowledge domains where the information situation can be modeled in detail with considerable validity can information advantage be estimated. However, that argument does not negate the value of the concept or the general guidance that can be inferred from it.

Measuring an Information Advantage

Figure 49 portrays how the respective information positions of two competitors can be portrayed using a variety of information attributes.

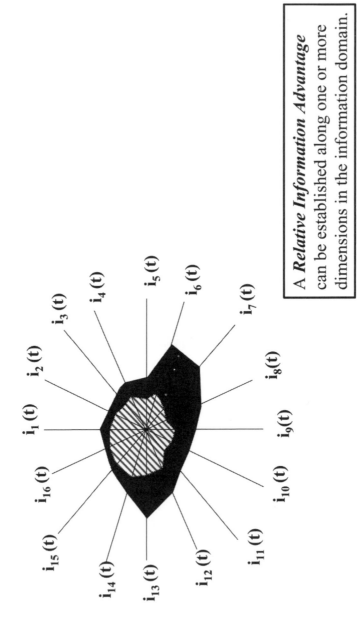

A *Relative Information Advantage* can be established along one or more dimensions in the information domain.

Figure 49. Information Domain: Measuring an Information Advantage

The information position of one competitor (Blue) is portrayed with the solid contour, and the information position of the second competitor (Red) is portrayed with the striped contour. It is clear from this graphic that a relative information advantage can be established along one or more axes. It is not difficult to envision a situation where Red dominates Blue on some axes, Red dominates on other axes, and the remaining axes are a draw.

Creating realistic examples of this type, in which the key attributes of information reach, richness, and quality of interaction are operationalized and the information pictures of adversaries composed, would be a valuable contribution to our understanding of Information Age Warfare. Analyses of well-understood historical cases might provide valuable insights, but systematic experimentation and well-constructed wargaming will be needed if this crucial issue is to be understood in light of current and potential technologies.

---

[1]Headquarters Effectiveness Assessment Tool "HEAT" User's Manual (McLean, VA: Defense Systems, Inc., 1984).

[2]The SIAP, defined in the Theater Missile Defense Capstone Requirements Document (TMD CRD), is the product of fused, common, continual, unambiguous tracks of airborne objects in the surveillance area. The SIAP provides the warfighter the ability to better understand the battlespace and employ weapons to their designated capabilities. The SIAP, a critical enabler of improved battlespace management and enhanced situational awareness, will feed the aerospace component of the Global Information Grid. The Department's effort to advance defense-wide efforts to improve joint battle force management and situational awareness falls under the responsibility of the SIAP System Engineering Task Force (SIAP SE). William S. Cohen, Secretary of Defense, *Annual Defense Report to the President and the Congress* (Washington, DC: January 2001).

CHAPTER 6

Cognitive Domain

Reference Model: Conceptual Framework

One of the key challenges facing commanders and their forces is developing an awareness of the situation as it exists in the physical domain, the information domain, and the cognitive domain. This process is two-sided, but focused on a single reality. The differing information domains of the two sides and their different cognitive orientations (worldviews, doctrine, etc.) guarantee cognitive awarenesses will differ. All contribute to a complex phenomenon we refer to as *the situation*, which is part reality, part information, and part cognition.

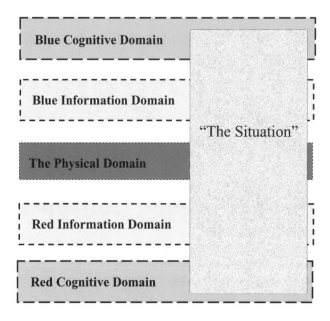

Figure 50. Reference Model: Conceptual Framework

Reference Model: The Situation

When the term *situational awareness* is used, it describes the awareness of a situation that exists in part or all of the battlespace at a particular point in time. In some instances, information on the trajectory of events that preceded the current situation may be of interest, as well as insight into how the situation is likely to unfold. The components of a situation are highlighted in Figure 51 and include missions and constraints on missions (e.g., ROE), capabilities and intentions of relevant forces, and key attributes of the environment. Relevant elements of the environment include: terrain, weather, social, political, and economic elements. For most military situations, time and space relationships (e.g., weapon ranges, rates of advance across different terrain) and the opportunities and risks relevant to the forces are also crucial elements.

• Awareness is a Perception of the Situation

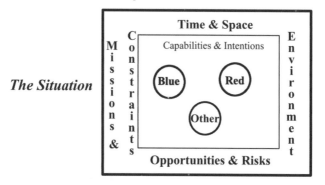

• Levels of Awareness
  – entities, relationships, the patterns and implications

Figure 51. Reference Model: The Situation

Battlespace Awareness

Battlespace Awareness is the result of the activities we undertake to enhance our information and protect it. Awareness *always* exists in the cognitive domain. It covers not what the information systems know, but what the people (commanders, key staff, etc.) know and are aware they know.

Figure 52 depicts the view to be provided for a U.S. Army Force XXI Brigade commander. Information consistent with the picture seen by this commander will also be available to others in the battlespace. This is the concept we call a common operational picture.

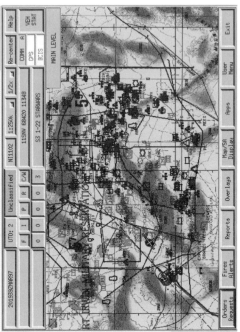

Figure 52. Battlespace Awareness

Note that the forces are not lined up, and that a FEBA (or forward edge of the battle area) is a concept that has limited meaning in this environment. In fact, the forces are intertwined with enemy forces, much as civilians and neutrals currently are intertwined in Kosovo. Hence, the potential for the commander's awareness to be incomplete or failure to recognize important differences is a significant element distinguishing the information system from awareness.

Reference Model: Components of Situational Awareness

As illustrated in Figure 53, when a human in the battlespace develops situational awareness, this awareness is developed in the cognitive domain. For example, a Tactical Action Officer standing watch on a U.S. Navy Ship in the Persian Gulf develops situational awareness by combining real-time information with knowledge that he or she has acquired as a result of operational experience. In this situation, relevant knowledge would consist of the capabilities of other nations' sea and air forces (e.g., Iran), as well their tactics, techniques, and procedures. In addition, within the cognitive domain, there are patterns and relationships that the human has developed to help make sense of complex situations.

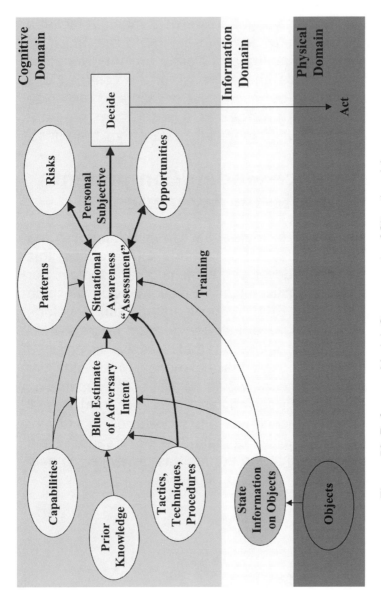

Figure 53. Reference Model: Components of Situational Awareness

The fusion of information and knowledge enables the watch officer to perform pattern recognition and to continually update an estimate of an adversary's intent, as well as make and maintain a real-time assessment of risks and opportunities.

With network-centric operations, state information on objects in the information domain can be shared between platforms. This ability to share information can play a key role in increasing both awareness and the degree to which it is shared. As Figure 54 illustrates, shared awareness typically involves sharing information and shared knowledge, and may be supported by a variety of information media (e.g., voice, data, and imagery).

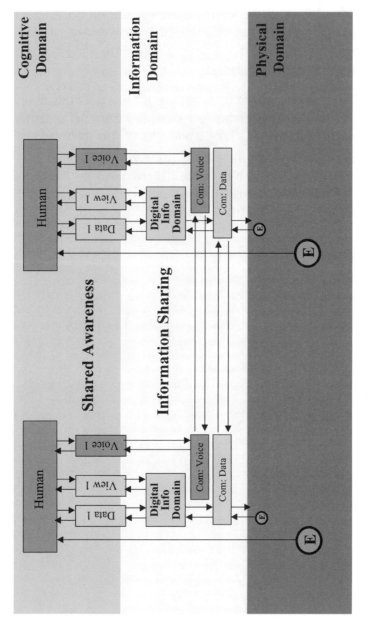

Figure 54. Shared Awareness

Shared Awareness

Shared awareness can be achieved in many ways, as is depicted in Figure 55. For example, as in Case 1, two individuals can both independently observe the same object or event in the physical domain; or, as in Case 2, they can both have access to independent sensor information regarding an object or event. Another way would be for one person to have observed an event and passed the information to another person, as in Case 3. Finally, as depicted in Case 4, independent sensor observations are shared and the fused results are available to two individuals.

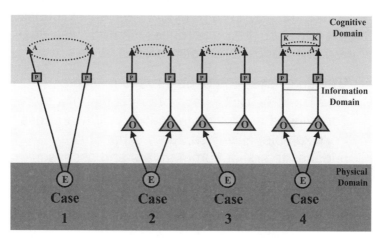

Figure 55. Achieving Shared Awareness

When, as in Case 4, the participants not only receive the same information, but also have an opportunity to discuss it or use it together in collaboration, the awareness may be both shared and enriched. This enrichment occurs when they process the information in the context of other relevant information or prior knowledge. In this case, the shared awareness achieved is more than simple common understandings but extends to new inferences. The value of collaboration (working together to solve a problem or produce a product) lies in this capacity to create higher knowledge and understanding in order to organize more effective and efficient activities.

Measurement and Assessment

The cognitive domain presents special problems in measurement and assessment. We have very limited and very intrusive tools to observe cognitive activities. For all practical purposes, we are limited to observing behaviors and asking commanders and staff to provide information about their awareness, shared awareness, shared knowledge, and collaboration.

- Traditional systems of observation, such as HEAT and ACCES, have proven able to capture behaviors that provide indications of awareness. For example, HEAT captures situational briefings to senior commanders and assesses their information quality. HEAT and ACCES also capture some qualities of interaction such as the number of staff sectors participating in planning.[1]

- RAND's Arroyo Center has recently published efforts to create new means of Information Superiority within the land warfare arena.[2]

- The Command Post of the Future program in DARPA has pioneered measuring situation awareness by systematic debriefing of participants in command center experimentation.[3]

- Recent work sponsored by ONR has identified four dimensions for the content of/and evaluating collaborative processes on conflict.[4]

Continuing combinations of innovative metrics and tried-and-true methods will be needed if we are to capture the cognitive dimensions of Information Age Warfare.

---

[1]Headquarters Effectiveness Assessment Tool "HEAT" User's Manual (McLean, VA: Defense Systems, Inc., 1984). Richard E. Hayes, T.A. Hollis, Richard L. Layton, W.A. Ross, and J.W.S. Spoor, "Enhancements to the Army Command and Control Evaluation System Task 1 Final Report" (FT Leavenworth, KS: U.S. Army Research Institute, 1993). *Headquarters Effectiveness Program Summary Task 002*, prepared for C3 Architecture and Mission Analysis, Planning, and Systems Integration Directorate, Defense Communications Agency (McLean, VA: Defense Systems, Inc., September 1983).

[2]Richard Darilek, Walter Perry, Jerome Bracken, John Gordon, and Brian Nichiporuk, *Measures of Effectiveness for the Information-Age Army* (Santa Monica, CA and Arlington, VA: RAND, 2001).

[3]John E. Kirzl, Diana G. Buck, and Jonathan K. Sander, "Operationalizing the AIAA COBP for Joint C2 Experimentation," *Proceedings of the Command and Control Research and Technology Symposium 2000* (Monterey, CA: June 2000).

[4]David Noble, Diana Buck, and Jim Yeargain, "Metrics for Evaluation of Cognitive-Based Collaboration Tools," *Proceedings of the 6th International Command and Control Research and Technology Symposium 2001* (Annapolis, MD: June 2001).

CHAPTER 7

Command and Control

Focus

N ew ways of thinking about command and control (C2) are at the heart of Information Age Warfare. As used here, the term C2 applies to the organizations, people, processes, and systems that enable commanders to understand a situation and provide intent, plans, and/or direction. The term C4ISR has evolved from C2 to emphasize the important role that communications, computers, intelligence, surveillance, and reconnaissance play in C2.

This section is organized into two elements: a discussion of how Information Age C2 differs from (but remains anchored in) the traditional approach and an analysis of C2 organizations and the key role of commander intent and C2 philosophy embedded in it.

Traditional View of Command and Control Processes: the OODA Loop

John Boyd introduced the Observe, Orient, Decide, and Act (OODA) loop in order to support analysis of pilot decisionmaking at a tactical level.[1] The idea (illustrated in Figure 56) is that decisions begin by observing the physical domain and are then placed in the context of other information and prior knowledge in order to orient the individual (or place the observations in context so they become useful information), which (in turn) allows the individual to decide what is to be done and act accordingly. The concept has proved to have considerable intuitive appeal and has been used for decades as the basis of both analysis and training. The phrase "turning inside the enemy's OODA loop," while originating in air-to-air combat, has become the shorthand way of understanding that speed of C2 process can provide advantage in combat situations.

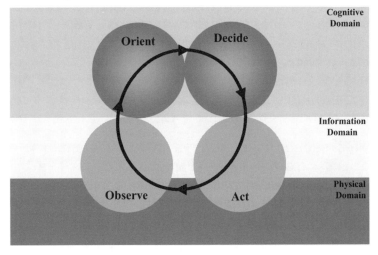

Figure 56. Traditional View of C2: OODA Loop

In our language, the act of observation must begin in the physical domain, may pass through some fusion with other observations, and is brought to the individual's attention through the information domain. The process of orientation occurs in the cognitive domain as the information content of the observations is internalized and placed in the context of the individual's prior knowledge, experience, and training. This is seen as providing the basis for a decision— also a cognitive activity. Finally, the decision itself must pass through the information domain (the controls of an aircraft, the directives of a commander) in order to become the basis for action.

The OODA loop has proven seductively robust and has been applied not only to pilot's activities in air-to-air combat, but also to organizational behavior at all levels. In our view, this is an error. As we discuss below, the OODA loop both oversimplifies the command and control process in ways that confound analysis and also reifies military organizations— implying that they have a single mind and make a single, coordinated decision across echelon and function. We believe that the OODA loop is outdated because it fails to differentiate crucial elements of the C4ISR process that must be considered in Information Age analyses.

Moreover, the OODA loop greatly oversimplifies the joint hierarchical model underlying military operations. Figure 57 places the cyclical OODA loop process into the larger context of joint operations. The five levels of command normally involved in U.S. joint operations have been shown as a hierarchy, with the National Command Authority (NCA) superior to a Commander in Chief (CINC), which in turn controls a Joint Task Force (JTF) made up of warfare arena Joint Force Component Commanders (JFCC) that are made up of the units that carry out the taskings within the operation. While there is only one NCA and one supported CINC controlling the operation (other supporting CINCs are normally involved, but not pictured here), major operations often involve more than one JTF and almost always involve multiple Joint Force Components and units. Maritime, Air, Land, and Special Forces are the traditional components. For simplicity's sake (the graphic is, in any case, very busy) each level of command is shown only once, and each is assumed to be located at a single site.

Time moves from left to right. The small OODA loops indicate decision cycles at the different echelons of command. The other symbols indicate C2 activities, which have been grouped into operations, logistics, and intelligence functions. For example, symbols containing M's indicate monitoring activity, or reports from the physical domain. Symbols containing P's indicate planning activities. Arrowheads indicate spot reports moving between command centers.

The frequency of all these C2 activities increased as you move down from the NCA level toward the unit level. Given that there are also many units and multiple JFCCs, these frequency differences become massive. The smaller number of decision cycles at the senior levels implies that they must look further into the future during each of their decision cycles.

The functional specialization (here simplified to operational, logistic, and intelligence) has also traditionally led to stovepipes (or specialized systems that link only selected elements of the C4ISR arena), to interoperability problems that make it difficult for functional specialists to share information even when they want to, and also to situations where information is available to different command centers and elements within the same command center. Hooking these

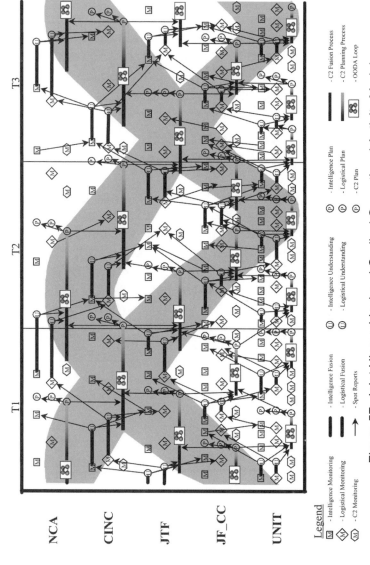

NCA

CINC

JTF

JF_CC

UNIT

T1   T2   T3

Legend

- Intelligence Monitoring
- Logistical Monitoring
- C2 Monitoring

- Intelligence Fusion
- Logistical Fusion
- Spot Reports

- Intelligence Understanding
- Logistical Understanding

- Intelligence Plan
- Logistical Plan
- C2 Plan

- C2 Fusion Process
- C2 Planning Process
- OODA Loop

Figure 57. Joint Hierarchical and Cyclical Operational Activity Model

systems together, particularly because the time cycles appropriate to different systems are quite different, almost guarantees that the elements of the force will have serious problems coordinating their efforts. The shaded waves in this figure highlight the fact that the information available to senior headquarters and the guidance provided by those senior headquarters has traditionally been temporally misaligned, contributing to the fog and friction of war.

An Information Age View of Traditional C4ISR Processes

Figure 58 provides an Information Age view of the traditional C4ISR process as it has been understood for several decades. However, it uses much richer constructs than those in the OODA loop. In this approach, C4ISR is seen as an adaptive control system seeking to influence selected aspects of an operating environment. That adaptive control system is supported by a variety of information systems. This C4ISR process is made up of half a number of interacting parts:

- Battlespace Monitoring

- Awareness

- Understanding

- Sensemaking

- Command Intent

- Battlespace Management

- Synchronization

• Information Systems

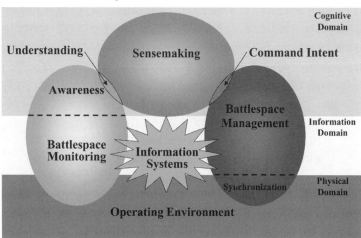

Figure 58. Traditional C4ISR Process

Operating Environment

The operating environment includes everything outside of the C4ISR processes and the systems that support them. The physical environment (terrain, weather, etc.) is one key dimension. Adversary forces form another. Own forces, to the extent that they are not part of C4ISR processes, are also in the environment. They represent the most controllable factors in the environment, but even they are imperfectly controllable due to the fog and friction of war. Other, neutral forces may also be present in the portion of the operating environment of interest. Their potential involvement or interference must also be considered. The operating environment also includes a host of political, social, and economic factors and actors, ranging from refugee populations to the infrastructure (communications, transportation, etc.) in the area.

Command at any level does not exist in isolation from a higher authority. The assigned mission and mission constraints also form part of the operating environment. The overall mission of a force is typically assigned by a political authority—the National Command Authority in the United States, but possibly some other entity like the UN or NATO when coalition warfare, peace operations or humanitarian missions are involved. Mission statements often include constraints such as rules of engagement or geographic limitations. While a military commander often influences the mission assigned and may be able to negotiate over the mission constraints, this is an arena where they do not have the final word.

Battlespace Monitoring

The process of monitoring the battlespace is the first part of the C4ISR process. This process starts in the physical domain with sensings (radar returns, satellite images, etc.) and reports (e.g., observations by scouts or units in contact). Imbedded in the information domain elements of this process are the fusion mechanisms by which data are stored, retrieved, and shared; data are placed in context and converted into information; and information is aggregated to form new knowledge or combined with previously documented knowledge (for example, adversary order of battle), as well as where coherent descriptions and pictures of the battlespace are developed and displayed.

Battlespace, as used here, refers to whatever mission environment the organization is working within, including humanitarian assistance, peace operations, counter-drug operations, or traditional combat. Monitoring includes information about all aspects of the operation—intelligence, own force status and activities, weather, terrain, and so forth. The quality of battlespace monitoring is reflected in the quality and age of the available information. This is the domain where information richness, reach, and quality of reach are most easily seen in the C4ISR process.

Awareness

Awareness exists only in the cognitive domain. It deals with what is "between the ears" after passing through perceptual filters. Those perceptions of the military situation will be strongly affected by the prior knowledge and belief systems that the people in the system bring from their education, training, and experience.

Battlespace awareness is not what is on the display, rather it is what is in one's head. Battlespace awareness is not static but a rich, dynamic comprehension of the military situation and the factors that drive it. High quality awareness is complete (includes the relevant information and actors), current, correct (does not include wrong information), and consistent (does not differ from one command center in the C4ISR system to another). Good battlespace awareness also envisions more than one potential future and recognizes uncertainty as a key element of the military situation.

Traditional C4ISR analyses have not differentiated the information domain from the cognitive domain or the process of battlespace monitoring from the awareness achieved. Data and information delivered to a command center were assumed to be known to all the individuals and organizations engaged in the C4ISR processes. Failures due to misperceptions or failures to incorporate new information were not considered. When such failures occurred, they were seen as aberrations and errors in the C2 process and not the products of a cross-domain transfer. Difficulties in generating shared awareness given the differing backgrounds, experiences, roles, and responsibilities of those involved in C4ISR processes continue to pose a major problem.

Understanding

Understanding—the comprehensive knowledge of the military situation—is both the last element in battlespace awareness and the first element in sensemaking. There is ample evidence that understanding a situation is the beginning of sensemaking. Experts typically jump directly from classifying a situation into the solution space(s) that can be used to control or resolve it. Indeed, empirical research into both real-world military decisionmaking and exercises have shown frequent use of a commander's shortcut, by which an experienced commander with confidence in his knowledge of a situation bypasses formal decision processes to match the patterns arising from battlespace monitoring, awareness, and understanding to directly select a course of action and begin planning for its implementation. Thus, understanding straddles awareness and sensemaking.

Some choices may be hard wired in the brain, a sort of conditioned reflex. Even when this does not occur and a more reflective decision process is employed, the understanding often forms or shapes the basis for developing and analyzing alternatives. Indeed, empirical analysis of hundreds of real and exercise decision cycles has shown that the quality of the understanding achieved is the single best predictor of the likelihood good decisions will be made and the military mission will be accomplished. That evidence cuts across the tactical and operational levels of command. Understandings are clearly in the cognitive domain, but can be shared through interactions in the information domain in the form of discussions, reports, plans, statements of command intent, and other written documents.

Sensemaking

Once an understanding of a situation that requires attention has been reached, individuals and organizations engage in a process best understood as *sensemaking*, in which they relate their understanding of the situation to their mental models of how it can evolve over time, their ability to control that development, and the values that drive their choices of action. In essence, they seek to accomplish three interrelated activities—generating alternative actions intended to control selected aspects of the situation, identifying the criteria by which those alternatives are to be compared, and conducting the assessment of alternatives. These three steps can be the subject of very formal staff processes or as simple as one officer examining a situation and making up his mind. When the decisions to be made are composed of well understood alternatives and explicit criteria for choosing (simple decisions) the process may be rapid and the error rate low for well trained officers. However, many military problems involve considerable uncertainty and novel features that require creative thought all the way from generating alternatives through the evaluation process. While supported by information and information systems, sensemaking takes place in the cognitive domain.

Research conducted on individual and group sensemaking, decisonmaking under stress, and small group decisionmaking has generated some guidelines that have also been validated by work on military decisionmaking. For example, all other things being equal, complex decisions are best made by small numbers of individuals who have different backgrounds and views of the situation. The more individuals who participate in a complex decision, the longer the process takes. Similarly, networks or multiconnected systems of communication are associated with better complex decisions but are slower than hierarchical structures.

Good sensemaking will also have examined the dynamics expected in the battlespace if each alternative is chosen. For example, likely enemy reactions to each alternative should be considered. Similarly, analyses should probe for key assumptions and dependencies in each course of action. In addition, good analyses look ahead, linking planned engagements together into a campaign and military activities into rich sets of political-military goals. However, these formal, structured analytic processes are often performed rapidly, even subconsciously by individuals. Given that military organizations typically require coordinated activities by a number of individuals or component organizations, shared sensemaking becomes a crucial part of the C4ISR process.

Command Intent

In contrast to the logic in the simpler OODA loop construct, which sees the output of the cognitive processes as a decision, or a choice among alternatives, the Information Age C4ISR process is understood to generate a richer product—command intent. This choice of language has two important, direct implications. First, the product is much richer than a choice among alternatives. In most command centers the results of sensemaking is high level guidance, but is far from a detailed plan. These products typically take the overall form and outline of a plan—specifying the objectives to be achieved, the major organizations involved, the general responsibilities of each, linkages among and schemes of maneuver for those organizations, and major constraints on them. These items will have formed the focus of the sensemaking discussion when courses of action were developed and assessed. Second, more than one individual is involved. Realistically, the commander's intent of traditional perspectives is replaced today by an intent that arises from dialogue between commanders and key staff at more than one level.

Like understanding, command intent is a linking function in the military C4ISR process—both the last step in sensemaking and the first step in battle management. It occurs in the cognitive domain, but is communicated through the information domain.

Synchronization

When command intent is established, a process designed to synchronize effects is initiated. Its goals are to reflect the intent in a plan, to disseminate that plan promptly and clearly, to monitor its implementation, and to support timely recognition of the need for either adjustments to the plan or the initiation of a new C4ISR cycle.

Military plans take many forms (from verbal directives to lengthy written documents with elaborate annexes). However, at their core, they always specify five things:

- What is to be accomplished (the military mission or missions assigned to subordinates);

- What assets (forces) are to be used, including command arrangements (who commands whom, who has priority, etc.);

- Schedules (which may involve specific times [e.g., jump off at 0430] or sequences [take Hill 472 and be prepared to attack Northwest on order to cut the enemy's lines of communication]);

- Boundaries (who is responsible for which geographic and functional area); and

- Contingencies (recognized situations in which changes to one or more of the previous four items are appropriate).

Plans are converted into directives, which must be clear and disseminated in time for subordinate organizations to prepare their own plans and organize their efforts. These plans also typically include specific elements intended to ensure battlespace awareness as they are implemented and permit adjustments as the situation develops over time.

Information Systems

In the traditional adaptive control, cyclic decision cycle, the information systems were very specialized. For example, intelligence systems have been separated from the C2 systems both to improve security and because these two different functions would interfere with each other's use of the limited bandwidth and computing power available in the theater of operations. Similarly logistics, personnel, and other combat support functions developed specialized communications and information systems so they could maintain data files and conduct their portion of the operation without being in the way of the command networks.

These differentiated information systems are represented in Figure 56 by the irregular spikes that penetrate the environment, effects synchronization, decisionmaking, and battlespace awareness functions.

Summary of Traditional C4ISR Process

In summary, the traditional C4ISR process was cyclic and designed to achieve adaptive control over selected aspects of the environment. Those aspects varied with the military mission: from denying an enemy key territory to inflicting casualties, to creating a stable security environment in peace enforcement missions or delivering food, water, shelter, and medicine in humanitarian crises. This process almost guarantees difficulties arising from disjoint decision cycles and differing information across time, space, and echelon of command. Information Age systems, combined with new ways of thinking about C4ISR that are enabled by them, offer major opportunities to reengineer the entire process.

C4ISR Today

As Figure 59 indicates, the primary changes in C4ISR implemented today deal with the information systems.

Decades of efforts, in some ways arising from the experiences in Grenada, have begun to increase interoperability and break down stovepipe communications systems. These processes have been hastened by changing information technologies. The massive increases in storage, computational power, and bandwidth over the past two decades have enabled greater sharing of data, information, and images. Improved sensors, new collection platforms (from satellites to UAVs), and improved fusion algorithms and approaches enabled by greater computing power have combined to increase battlespace awareness and reduce uncertainty in many contexts.

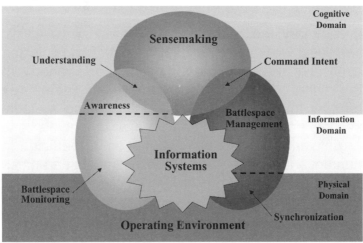

Figure 59. C4ISR Process Today

Less impact has been felt in decisionmaking and battle management. Concepts like "ring of fire" and Network Centric Warfare point the way to greater reliance on systems which support these functions, but the real-world systems being employed have not yet either achieved the needed levels of precision and reliability or been embraced by the forces in the field.

While the information systems have penetrated more deeply into each of the key functional arenas, their impact on doctrine, organizational structures, tactics, techniques, and procedures has been minimal. For example, analysis of the NATO operation in Bosnia, undertaken by the NATO Joint Assessment Team (JAT), showed that staff work was heavily dominated by PowerPoint presentations created in traditional functional structures, rather than integrated data and information sets. Similarly, the first exercise conducted by CINCPAC in its new command center during April 2000 used traditional staff structures—J-1 through J-6, supplemented by a Crisis Action Team (CAT). Collaboration technologies were employed within the J-4 functional area to link logistics personnel on the CAT floor with their reach-back teams with access to the detailed databases needed to coordinate efforts in the theater.

All the Services continue to conduct exercises and experiments to explore the use of self-reporting systems (platforms that generate information about their location, fuel status, ammunition, and need for repair), collaboration tools that link staffs across function and echelon of command, and new ways to exchange information within the battlespace (linking sensors to shooters, for example), but none have yet implemented more than incremental changes in their fielded systems.

Even though the progress has been limited, and limited largely to linear extensions of old practices, C4ISR has already begun to improve. The Kosovo operation, while hardly perfect, was more efficient (fewer sorties for more delivered weapons) and demonstrated greater ability to control forces in the field than has been previously possible. Tools such as video teleconferencing and broader bandwidth for sharing more information, if only in the form of PowerPoint slides, have increased the speed and consistency of understandings and led to richer decisionmaking. Similarly, decision processes have become faster and have generated a more common grasp of what is to be done—speeding and improving the quality of battle management.

Greater Integration

The future of C4ISR lies in greater integration. As shown in Figure 60, this integration will occur over time, space, function, and echelon. Moreover, it will occur because the information systems cease to be outside the C4ISR processes and become embedded in them. This networked C4ISR process will differ not only in degree (more data, information and knowledge, better integrated and available to more actors in more different forms) but also in kind. The very nature of the C4ISR process will be transformed, which will have massive implications for doctrine, organization, and training.

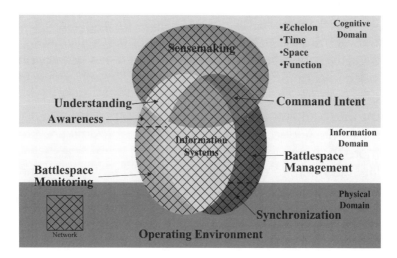

Figure 60. Greater Integration

Integration Across Echelon

This is the most advanced element of the changes taking place. The same types of technology that allow people to share information, collaborate and search intelligently on the Internet are also becoming available for battlespace awareness and management. As is typical of innovations, this one has taken hold first within traditional organizations and structures. Hence, the intelligence community has begun to rely on SIPRNET, a simple, but secure, analogy to the Internet. However, even this simple advance has naturally grown to include intelligence cells at customer sites (CINCs, Joint Task Forces, etc.)—speeding access to new information and making cross-talk easier. Moreover, as a secure environment, SIPRNET has also attracted a variety of non-intelligence users. Similarly, the ubiquitous Microsoft Office software and PowerPoint presentation slides have made it easier to share the information offered to commanders. Video technologies have also emerged as tools for creating rich linkages between senior headquarters. U.S. planning for politically sensitive operations such as Haiti has relied heavily on video teleconferencing to link senior military officers with one another and with the political leaders, particularly on the complex issue of defining appropriate military missions. Video from UAVs can also be delivered to more than one level of command simultaneously. Rich linkages across echelons have also developed in the combat service support functions such as logistics (movement and sustainment), personnel, and managing medical support.

As rich as these systems are today, they will mature into richer linkages over time. In a richly integrated system, planning will be virtually simultaneous across echelons of command. In fact, the current mapping of echelon with level of war is in the process of change. With these unlinked, the meaning of echelons will undoubtedly change.

The system today, illustrated earlier in Figures 57 and 58, requires subordinate echelons to wait for plans from higher echelons before they can undertake the detailed planning and physical actions required to implement the plans from senior headquarters. A system of warning orders is used to inform subordinate headquarters of the kinds of mission changes being considered so they can comment or begin rough planning. In the future, computational power and bandwidth will exist to involve multiple echelons directly in the initial thinking throughout collaborative processes. This will mean a richer battlespace awareness, a more rapid and effective decisionmaking process, and more agile and better focused battle management. Commanders will be able to use collaborative tools that can both speed up and better integrate their plans as well as provide greater lead time and richer understanding of the commander's intent at all levels.

Integration Across Function

While some progress has been made in this area, the greatest gains are yet to come. Recent developments have primarily focused on breaking down stovepipes so that the specialists in different functions can have access to a common operational picture. This thinking has now extended to a common *relevant* operational picture, which means they can each have tailored information based on the same underlying data, information, and knowledge bases.

Experimental efforts have also been made so that key platforms will be self-reporting—their locations, fuel status, ammunition status, maintenance posture, damage, and other key features are known to a common database. This primarily assists battlespace management by linking current operations to logistics and sustainment functions. However, currently these systems are neither reliable enough nor secure enough to support real-world operations, nor are they joint. Research and development continue, with great promise, but limited scope.

Network Centric Warfare concepts push information technologies even further—using networked information to directly link sensors to shooters and precision munitions to deliver weapons at stand-off ranges that minimize the risks to friendly forces. This approach can, if the information generated is of high enough quality and integrated rapidly enough, permit very agile operations using emergent behaviors or self-synchronized forces to accomplish missions. These concepts dramatically alter the C4ISR processes—turning hierarchical centralized structures into dinosaurs, enabling collaboration across functional arenas, and making senior commands primarily responsible for creating the conditions necessary for their subordinates to be successful.

Greater Integration and Implied Decision Types

The impact of this level of integration transforms the decisionmaking process. On the one hand, a whole set of decisions emerges where, given adequate quality and currency of information, and confidence in that quality and currency, the decisions are obvious. In other words, to know is to both decide and to act. These are *automatable* decisions on Figure 61. For them, any distinctions among battlespace awareness, decisionmaking, and battle management are artificial. These decisions can be automated, at least under particular rules of engagement. For example, theater ballistic missile defense during war is likely to be fully automatic and may have to be in order to work quickly enough to be successful. These can occur by simply linking observations from the physical domain to preset algorithms or rules in the information domain.

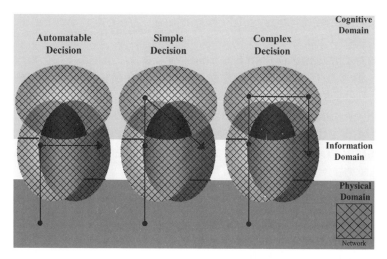

Figure 61. Greater Integration and Implied Decision Types

Simple decisions, on the other hand, are those for which the set of appropriate choices are fully known and articulated, and the criteria by which selections will be made among them are also understood, although some human judgment is required. For example, contingency plans are typically designed around well understood conditions, but a human is required to (a) ensure the conditions have occurred (and that the information about them is correct and reliable), and (b) decide that the circumstances are similar enough to those envisioned when the contingency plan was designed that the action remains appropriate. These decisions are also based on observations from the physical domain and processed in the information domain, but must involve human cognition before they can be made. These are the simplest sensemaking cases because they involve recognition of patterns that have been imbedded in prior knowledge.

Doctrine, tactics, and procedures are often written in order to transform otherwise complex decisions into simple decisions in the field. While a commander may have an infinite number of maneuvers that can be made in given circumstances, doctrine will organize them into a few alternatives (vertical envelopment, flanking movement, etc.) and provide criteria for selecting the correct class of maneuver across a wide range of situations.

Complex decisions are common in military affairs and involve having to (a) create the set of relevant options, (b) identify the criteria by which they will be compared, and (c) specify the process or method by which a decision will be made. This last step involves deciding how the information related to criteria will be integrated, including not only weightings, but also the role of uncertainty. The formal course of action analysis approach taught in military schools is designed to help senior commanders with complex decisions. C4ISR processes and systems cannot do anything more than provide support to complex decisions. Capabilities such as rapidly, currently, and correctly providing responses to the Commander's Critical Information Requirements (CCIRs) and generating rich visualizations that both integrate information from a wide variety of sources and also focus the commander and key staff on the crucial decisions required in the battlespace will be required. Note that even in complex decisions there is some very real overlap between the five key C4ISR functions: battlespace monitoring, awareness, understanding the military situation, the sensemaking process, developing command intent, and battle management.

Perhaps most significantly, new collaboration technologies will make it possible to consult with functional experts, commanders and staffs at all levels and at distant locations, and existing data or knowledge bases rapidly and efficiently. Complex decisions are those where collaboration has been shown, in laboratory research and some military exercises, to be most likely to improve decision quality.

Integration Over Time

The natural consequence of the tighter integration across function and echelon is greater integration over time. As the currency of battlespace monitoring and awareness improves, the length of time required to recognize that a change in command intent is needed declines, while the opportunity to see decision requirements ahead of time increases. Similarly, as decision transparency increases due to the network, the distinction between command intent and execution blurs and these processes become merged. Rather than seeking to create command intent that will last a long time in order to give subordinates an opportunity to plan for and execute them properly, the C4ISR process is postured to make many interrelated decisions that form a coherent whole and can be rapidly updated at irregular times depending on situational development. As the need for hierarchical coordination declines, the potential for collaboration and coherent patterns of action across echelons and functions increases. This increased speed results in improved agility and adaptability. Obvious indicators that this integration is occurring are increasing numbers of contingencies within the plans, focused information or intelligence requirements that enable the force to recognize the conditions identified in those contingency plans, and more rapid adjustments when important developments occur in the battlespace. In essence, a better adaptive control system is created and more self-synchronization is enabled.

Integration Across Geography

The extension of the argument to greater integration across geographic space should be obvious. Fewer control measures (boundaries of action) are required because all the units are aware of the locations, status, and actions of the others. For the same reason, providing support across distance becomes easier. For example, an overhead sensor may be able to provide general location information for a target that is used to vector a UAV to get more precise location information and guide a stand-off weapon to the target. While these assets have historically been controlled by different command centers, their use of a common network enables the sensor-to-shooter function to be supported with little regard to who owns the sensor, the shooter, or which piece of the battlespace. Similarly, ground units fighting near the seam between commands will be able to coordinate their tactics as though they had a common commander.

At higher levels of command (operational, for example), this greater integration across geography will simplify creating a coherent understanding of the battlespace and its dynamics, enable coherent sensemaking that links adjacent and multiple echelon command intent and plans into a coherent whole, and enable much more agile and responsive synchronization of effects. In particular, the ability to tie different types of forces and weapons (from direct fire to information weapons) into a coherent package will be greatly enhanced. Hence the greater integration will occur both in the information domain and in the cognitive domain. However, the most valuable impact will be greater synchronization of actions and hence effects.

Overall Change

Figure 62 illustrates the overall integration that can be anticipated. As the C4ISR system becomes network-centric, integration will naturally occur across geographic space, over time, across echelons of command, and across functional arenas. Obviously, this will transform the structure of the C4ISR system and process into one dependent on the capacity to collaborate, and often to one that will depend on self-synchronization. Done well, this can be foreseen to generate much faster C4ISR as well as more effective military forces. All this assumes, of course, that the necessary technological investments are made and that the forces have personnel, training, and doctrine to exploit these advantages in information.

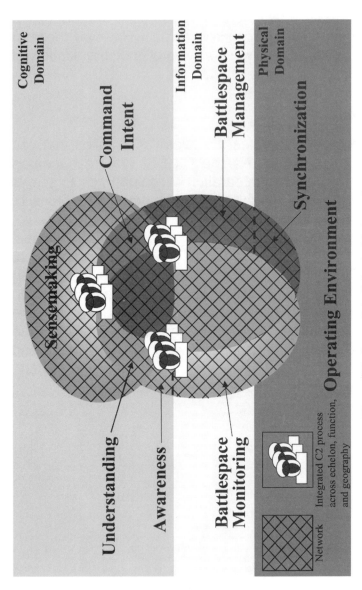

Figure 62. Overall Anticipated Integration

Vulnerabilities and Remaining Issues

Beyond the relatively simple questions of developing and integrating the technologies needed, two families of key issues must be addressed if network-centric C4ISR is to be as successful as envisioned. First, the quality of information needed for such a system must be made available. Second, adequate information assurance is necessary.

Information quality is crucial because the entire C4ISR process depends on correctly perceiving the military situation and in creating a common perception across all the actors. Not only must the situational monitoring be common, it must also be correctly perceived. These perceptions must not only be common and correct, but they must also be perceived as credible in the eyes of the users. If commanders and key staff perceive major uncertainties, they can be expected to (and as military commanders should) proceed cautiously, using their actions to develop better awareness and contingency plans to ensure agility as their knowledge of the battlespace changes with the receipt of new or corrected information. Moving from a world, as Van Creveld discusses, where the goal of the C4ISR systems is to *reduce uncertainty*, to one in which its principal function is to *exploit high quality information* assumes improved information and decisionmakers who believe that information. If the system fails to meet that need or to create confidence in its products, the process will not be transformed.

Similarly, information assurance is an essential assumption of these changes. If adversaries are able to capture or corrupt the information in the C4ISR system, both wrong-headed actions and paralysis of decisionmaking become distinct possibilities. Hence the integrity of the data and information systems become a primary concern and limit on the transformation of C4ISR.

Nothing we have said about the potential of technology should be understood to suggest either the removal of the element of uncertainty or a reduction in the role of the military commander and staff. Uncertainty will be a part of any foreseeable future battlespace. Better information technology and more integrated C2 processes should, however:

- Reduce the uncertainty;

- Help commanders and staffs be aware of and understand the residual uncertainty; and

- Take steps to overcome the effects of uncertainty.

Similarly, improved C4ISR should enable the commander and key staff to focus their time and attention on more complex problems and use their judgment and expertise more effectively.

In addition, the increased integration of future C4ISR should not be understood to suggest a lack of specialization. Indeed, some of the most advanced concepts for applying information technologies, such as "ring of fire" and Network Centric Warfare, actually envision more specialized sets of assets interacting in ways that allow synchronized effects. Admiral Arthur Cebrowski has argued, for example, that one implication of new information technologies is that unmanned sensors will be put at risk while personnel and fighting platforms are kept farther from harm.[2] Similarly, in OOTW the improved information systems capability makes it possible to more correctly assign responsibilities to appropriate specialized organizations (e.g., medical NGOs, NGOs providing food, host government agencies providing shelter, military forces providing security) and to synchronize their efforts over time and space. Indeed, better information technologies and more integrated C2 processes enable gains in both efficiency and effectiveness.

C2 Organization

Perhaps the most difficult aspect of C2 in the Information Age is the way it will alter C2 organizations. The military culture, both in the U.S. and in foreign militaries, is firmly anchored in a functionally decomposed structure, both in terms of fighting elements (the division of responsibilities across Services and within Services across branches such as armor and artillery on land or air, surface, and subsurface in naval warfare) and in terms of staff elements (personnel, intelligence, operations, etc.). These divisions are engrained in traditions, training, and experience. They represent a significant element of the military culture and the self-definition of many officers and non-commissioned officers. Hence, they will be resistant to change.

However, these current organizational decompositions are products of the technologies and information capabilities that were available to the military when they were developed. For example, weapons platforms have for generations carried their own sensors or depended on the five senses of their operators. In the Information Age, sensors can be decoupled from weapons platforms and, in many cases, from manned platforms. Hence, the sensors can be placed at risk, not the people. Organizationally, information from sensors can be made available to potential shooters far from the threat. In such circumstances, and particularly when the need for rapid reaction is crucial (targets are increasingly fleeting, stand-off weapons with terminal guidance are increasingly available, etc.), the artificial distinction between intelligence assets (sensors) and operations assets (shooters) makes little sense. Once priorities are set and the criteria for matching weapons to targets are understood (including the quality of the information available to ensure only the correct targets are served and collateral damage has been considered), the fewer organizational barriers to collaborative planning and synchronization of activities that remain, the better.

Change in C2 organization is crucial to achieving the benefits available in the Information Age. This can be expected to be a long pole in the tent because of the cultural impediments as well as the perceived high cost of getting it wrong. The very great difficulty of trying out novel organizational approaches (finding commanders and staffs who can undertake experimental approaches without creating problems with their current training and levels of skill, finding facilities that can support such tests, etc.) has already emerged as a practical issue. In the end, however, the full impact of Information Age concepts and technologies cannot be achieved without appropriate changes to C2 organization and empirical data collection in structured war games, exercises, and experiences. As argued earlier, human behavior is simply too complex to model or treat by assumption.

Organization can be understood as simply a number of entities, having specific responsibilities, and united for a common purpose. Note that the entities do not have to be different. For example, tank formations may deploy with some elements screening for others who are organized into a main battle force. On the other hand, typical military organizations are made up of quite specialized entities with functionally different, but interrelated, purposes. For example, theater air force elements include strike aircraft, escort aircraft with missions such as suppression and air-to-air interception, tankers, air control aircraft, photographic aircraft, and others.

Regardless of force composition, C2 organization should be understood to be the interaction between three very different aspects:

• The structure of the organization;

• The functional distribution of roles; and

• The capacity of the entities and systems that make up the C2 system.

Military organizational *structures* have traditionally been seen as hierarchical, with the distribution of authority identical to the distribution of information. Even today, formal correspondence intended for any member of a military command is addressed to the commanding officer of the organization (a practice that is disappearing as an Internet-based model of e-mail emerges as common practice). However, one immediate impact of Information Age Warfare has been to decouple the flow of information from the military hierarchy. As more and more networks have been introduced and stovepipes have been removed, the commander's role, and that of the headquarters, has been altered in very fundamental ways.

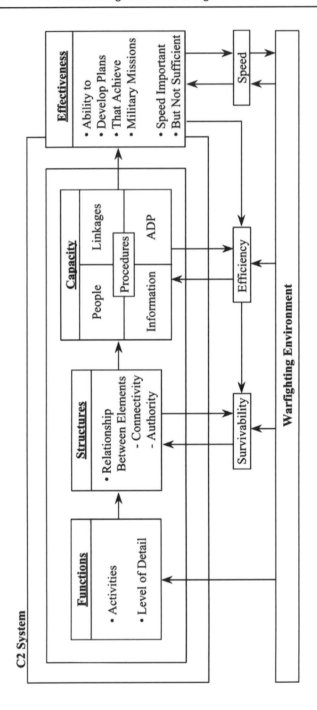

Figure 63. Structure, Function, Capacity, and Their Impacts

Perhaps more important in the long run, the principle that form follows function means that this new, less centralized information flow will inevitably lead to changes in the work patterns. Business process re-engineering in modern corporations is all about managing this process intelligently rather than having it emerge with unintended consequences. Military organizations are beginning to see changes in the way they do business as Information Age technologies become available and as Information Age concepts are adopted. But they are not always in control of this change. Some of the more business-like military functions, such as sustainment, scheduling long-haul transportation, and medical support, have begun to benefit from relatively straightforward adoption of new business models. However, the management of forces engaged in real-world missions is only beginning to experience these changes. Ultimately, major changes (flattening of organizations, including removal of whole levels of command; elimination of redundant functions, such as battle damage assessment in a battlespace that is constantly monitored; use of collaboration to enable integration; and automation of simple decisions) will occur. However, the issue remains open whether they will occur (a) as a result of deliberate choices by the U.S. military or as unintended consequences or (b) as a result of changes initiated by adversaries or efforts by the United States to capitalize on its Information Age potential.

The *distribution of functional roles* is the second way in which organizations differ. The classic description of a bureaucracy includes increasingly specialized elements with interlocking roles. Military structures have that feature. One way C2 organizations can be different is by adding new elements (e.g., a civil-military operations center to manage the interface with private voluntary organizations, non-governmental organizations, and international organizations), combining elements in new ways (merging the intelligence and own force monitoring functions into an information officer), or eliminating redundant or unnecessary functions.

However, functional differences also occur when commanders or headquarters are tasked to perform the same activities at different levels of detail. For example, Information Age senior headquarters are expected to generate more general directives that specify only missions or objectives and leave the details of how they are to be accomplished up to subordinate organizations. The sensor-to-shooter loop in which targets are serviced by assets from anywhere in the battlespace is a very simple form of this change. Given that target types have been prioritized and rules or algorithms exist to allocate weapons to targets, high quality information about targets can be processed within that guidance with no further action from the senior headquarters or the commander.

However, the structures and functions within a C2 organization must also be designed with the *capacity* of the C2 systems in mind. Capacity, as used here, is the ability to perform work. It varies with a number of factors including the inherent capabilities of the individuals in the organization, their training and experience, the processes and procedures they use, as well as the information processing and communications technologies available to support them. Taken together, these capacities enable the organization to perform at different levels of effectiveness and efficiency.

Note that the three key elements of C2 organization (structure, functions, and capacity) are highly interdependent. Hence, changing any one element or a significant part of an element will enable (and may require) changes in the others. Failure to make the three realms consistent will at least result in lost opportunities and may well reduce overall performance because the C2 system loses coherency. The primary impact of Information Age technologies on the military will not be their direct functionality, but rather the changes they enable in structure, function, and other aspects of capacity, as well as their impacts on the ability to accomplish missions.

Information Age military organizations will enable components to share knowledge and collaborate on key issues and plans, as well as synchronize their actions. However, in order to work together, these organizations will still require guidance. Part of that guidance can be developed independent of the mission in the form of shared prior knowledge: common education and training, doctrine, tactics, techniques, and procedures. However, the mission specific element of that guidance will be reflected in the specific commander's intent. This crucial element provides the *purpose* essential for individuals and entities to unite their efforts.

Commander's Intent

Commander's intent is a simple statement that goes beyond the mission to communicate how that mission is to be accomplished. It focuses on the decisive elements of how the mission is to be accomplished. At the same time, it is a very general statement, leaving room for initiative and interpretation by individual commanders. Establishing clear and meaningful commander's intent is at the heart of any C2 system. It provides the means for subordinate commanders and functional commands to focus their efforts. In essence, when everyone has a common understanding of the commander's intent, they are better able to make mutually supporting decisions.

This enables both the delegation of decisions and decisionmaking arenas. These can be contingencies (reactions to pre-established variations in the operating environment, such as the enemy force committing its reserve in a particular sector) or simply choices about the best way to achieve selected goals. In addition, clear commander's intent allows all the friendly actors to recognize circumstances that call for changes in plans or behaviors.

In order to be effective, the commander's intent must be established and disseminated very early in the process. Once it has been established, all the actors in the C4ISR system possess the essential understanding of how the organization will approach the problem and can work efficiently and effectively both individually and in collaboration. Changes in commander's intent mean fundamental changes in the way the overall organization behaves and must, therefore, be disseminated quickly and simultaneously throughout the military organization.

Approaches to C2

Two decades ago the Defense Information Systems Agency (DISA, at the time called the Defense Communications Agency) sponsored broad research on a variety of historical systems approaches to command arrangements,[3] including that of the United States (in WWII, Korea, Vietnam, and various crises), UK (in WWII and the modern period), the USSR (in WWII and the modern period), Israel (in 1956, 1967, and 1973), China (in the modern period), NATO, and others perceived to have effective military establishments. Lessons learned and changes made by outstanding commanders such as Eisenhower, Nimitz, and Bradley, as well as within significant commands (such as the 12th Air Force and the British Fighter Command during World War II), were also examined.

One product of that historical and comparative research was the identification of three major types of C2 approaches, each with at least two important subtypes. All six approaches have been successful, but each is more appropriate for some types of forces than others. Figure 64 shows these subtypes and the relative headquarter's capacity (information processing and military art capability) required to apply them successfully. The key distinction is the level of centralization required, ranging from the heavily distributed control-free to the inherently centralized cyclic approaches. The three categories of directive specificity reflect the level of detail required in the directives issued by headquarters in each type of system, ranging from mission-specific to objective-specific to order-specific.

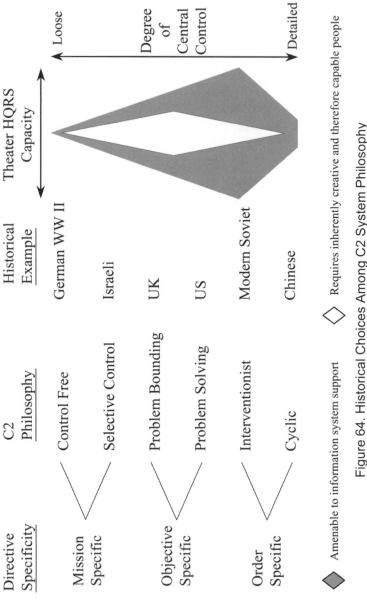

Figure 64. Historical Choices Among C2 System Philosophy

Control-free command centers (the most distributed approach) seek to assign missions to their subordinates, who are then expected to employ all the assets available to them to accomplish the missions. This requires a military organization where the lower echelons are competent and trusted implicitly by the higher echelons. The system designed by the Germans for World War II is the case that fits most clearly in this category. The success of Germany's *blitzkrieg* was due not only to the superior weapons and mobility of the German forces, but also to the capacity of their officers and non-commissioned officers to operate independently, even under trying conditions. (The fact that Hitler and the Nazi party often interfered with this system is one major reason that it did not work effectively all the time.) This idea approaches the self-synchronization concept in the current era.

The Israelis admired the philosophy of the German approach, but felt that it was perhaps too decentralized, particularly given their narrow margin for error in wars that threatened their national security. As a result, the Israelis have developed *selective-control* systems in which senior headquarters also issue mission-type orders and expect subordinates to take broad and deep initiatives. However, their senior headquarters follow the battle in detail and are *prepared* to intervene in the event of a major opportunity or major threat that the lower-level command does not perceive or cannot manage. This approach requires great discipline on the part of the senior commanders, who have tactical-level information and considerable skill as tactical commanders but only intervene when operational or strategic issues emerge. In essence, the Israelis prefer rapid reaction on the battlefield but seek to maintain the capability for central intervention.

Taken together, the control free and selective control systems comprise the more general class of *mission-oriented* command and control arrangements. Each level tends to assign missions to its subordinates and permit them to define further details of the military situation, beginning with selecting the objectives necessary to accomplish their missions. The presumption is that the commander on the scene has more current and accurate information than senior headquarters *and* has adequate resources to exploit local opportunities and protect the force while accomplishing the mission. This assumption is better in today's information-rich operating environment than it has been in the past. Lower-level commanders can benefit from information that has traditionally been held at higher levels and from direct feeds from platforms such as UAVs. Moreover, through a combination of doctrine, training, experience, and mission orders, the subordinate commander is presumed to understand the intent and overall concept of the operation of the senior commander so that local actions will not be inconsistent with the larger military mission or the actions of other commanders.

UK doctrine can best be understood as *problem-bounding*. That is, the senior headquarters tend to compose their directives in terms of the *objectives* to be accomplished but couch them in very general terms. Hence, directives are more specific than mere mission assignments and some explicit boundaries (deadlines for achieving some objectives, guidance on risks that might be accepted or avoided, etc.) are articulated.

British plans for an operation tend to be less detailed than those of Americans, often by a factor of three to one, reflecting this lack of detail.

For their parts, the U.S. Army and Navy have, since World War II, tended to issue *problem-solving* directives in which missions and objectives are articulated for two levels of subordinates and substantial guidance about how the objectives are to be achieved is also included. Although this approach provides more detailed direction than the British philosophy, considerable room remains for lower-level initiative and creativity in accomplishing the objectives. At the same time, however, the high-technology assets which U.S. forces tend to employ often mean that subordinates are heavily dependent on senior commanders for key assets such as lift, intelligence, supplies, and precision munitions.

Together the problem-bounding and problem-solving approaches comprise the *objective-oriented* approach to command arrangements. They assume some level of trust, creativity, and initiative in subordinate commands but stress synchronization of assets and actions. As a result, they assume greater coordination and more continuous contact between superior and subordinate and among subordinate commands. This provides greater control. These systems were brought to fruition by the resource-rich, in attrition wars, where superior material and technology were applied to wear down adversaries with limited resources (such as Axis powers in World War II).

Ultimately someone in every military system issues *orders* to subordinates (directives that tell units and people what to do, where to do it, how and when it is to be done). However, this is only done by headquarters above the tactical level in very centralized systems (or in cases where politically sensitive assets such as nuclear or chemical weapons are involved). These have historically been systems where the commanders at lower levels are considered weak, unable, or unlikely to take the initiative or develop effective courses of action on their own.

The Cold War era Soviet system, for example, can best be described as *interventionist*, in that it relied heavily on central authority to issue directives, but also maintained very detailed information about the battle (requiring continuous and specific reports from subordinates two layers down) and attempted centralized control through detailed directives. The Soviets used exercises and training of front line units to ensure that they could execute a variety of quite standard maneuvers, from breakthrough assaults and river crossings for land forces to standardized attack patterns against U.S. carrier battle-groups at sea. Senior headquarters specified the time and place for such preplanned operations and controlled them through the detailed preplanning process.

The greatest degree of centralization occurs, however, when the senior headquarters issues orders to all subordinates but does so on the basis of a preset cycle time. The Chinese Army and the Soviet World War II forces adopted this approach because their communications structures could not provide continuous information to the central headquarters and because their subordinate organizations were culturally unable to display initiative in the absence of detailed directives. The U.S. Air Force has followed the same approach since World War II, but for a very different reason—the complexity of air operations has meant the information required, coordination needed, and relative scarcity of the assets involved tend to drive the decisionmaking up the chain of command. The USAF has chosen to invest in communications systems so they can issue orders at the numbered Air Force level. The 24-hour air tasking order is *cyclic*, however, in part because the amount of processing needed to develop these intricate plans requires relatively long lead times. Flexibility is created in all tasking orders by creating a variety of on-call missions and by making adjustments "on the fly" by diverting aircraft from one specific mission to another, higher priority target, or mission.

The existence of these six distinct types of command and control systems in prominent military establishments helps to explain why coalition operations are plagued by interoperability problems at the cultural, organizational, and the procedural (doctrinal) levels, to say nothing of the technical communications systems they use. Successful joint and coalition operations will require adopting consistent command and control philosophies and creating command arrangements that enable elements of the force to operate coherently.

Capacity Requirements for Different Command Arrangements

Major differences exist in the capacities required for the six types of command arrangements. Figure 65 illustrates those differences.

Command Approach	Inputs		Processing	Outputs from Theatre HQ		Subordinate Attributes	
	Detail of Update	Frequency of Update	Quantity Required	Level of Detail	Frequency	Professional Competence	Creativity/ Initiative
Control-Free	Low	Low	Low	Low	Low	Very High	Very High
Selective Control	Low	Very High	Moderate/ Low	Low	Moderate/ Low	High	High
Problem-Bounding	Moderate	Moderate	Moderate	Moderate	Moderate	High/ Moderate	High/ Moderate
Problem-Solving	Moderate	Moderate	High/ Moderate	High/ Moderate	High/ Moderate	Moderate	Moderate
Interventionist	High	Very High	Very High	Moderate	High	Moderate/ Low	Moderate/ Low
Cyclic	High	Very Low	High/ Moderate	Very High	Very Low	Low	Very Low

Figure 65. Capacity Requirements for Different Command Arrangements

First, assuming that the quality of information provided is constant across all cases, *the more centralized the decisionmaking, the more information required at the senior headquarters*, which means greater detail in each report and situation update transmitted. However, major differences exist in the frequency with which updates are required. Control-free systems, in which the central commander is not seeking to control the schedule of events closely, require infrequent updates.

The two approaches that seek to issue objective-specific directives, problem-bounding and problem-solving, require moderately frequent updates. Cyclic command assumes periodic, paced updates, the lowest frequency. Interventionist and selective control systems, both seeking to assert themselves on an as-required basis, must have almost continuous updates about the situation, making the capacity required very high.

The information-processing capacity required for these different approaches also varies widely. This represents the effort needed to receive the appropriate inputs, transform them into information the C2 system can act on, and conduct the necessary operations to support decisionmaking. Because the volume of input and output to be processed is lowest for control-free systems, the processing capacity required is also low. This grows as the degree of centralization rises. However, cyclic approaches, because they have a low update rate, need less processing capacity than their interventionist counterparts, which must be ready to act at any time. In general, *greater capability to acquire, integrate, move, and process larger amounts of information rapidly makes more centralized decisionmaking possible.*

Indeed, current discussion of the need for new C2 approaches in an era of Information Age Warfare explicitly considers situations where the best (most current, accurate, and complete) information may no longer be located at the subordinate command engaged in the field, but rather may be located at senior headquarters. This implies a change in the best approach to C2, although considerable choice exists in how information is distributed using state-of-the-art technologies. The increasing need for reach-back capability and collaborative tools is a recognition of these changes. Whenever speed of decisionmaking becomes crucial, creation of automated approaches to decisionmaking becomes relevant.

The amount of internal information processing required is minimized in control-free systems and maximized in those systems seeking to issue orders from the top, particularly the interventionist model. The same pattern generally holds for the quantity of output generated and, therefore, the coordination and explanation of what is wanted. Here, however, the interventionist approach (as practiced by the Cold War era Soviets) is able to take advantage of pre-real-time learning by subordinates so it can, in essence, call plays like a football team and does not have to provide detailed instructions in every order. However, this approach limits the flexibility of the command system, making it difficult to make subtle adjustments in response to opportunities or threats on the battlefield.

Finally, the different command approaches require very different capacities among the subordinate commanders and their organizations. In general, *the more centralized the command arrangements, the less required from subordinates*. Competence here refers to the ability to plan, coordinate, and execute military functions. Similarly, *the less-centralized systems require more creativity and initiative on the part of subordinate commands.* In fact, classic cyclic systems (such as that of Stalinist Russia during World War II) are perceived to punish subordinate commands that undertake creative activities or move off the detailed orders or preplanned activities they are given.

The degree of centralization adopted also influences the degree to which automation can be used to achieve the capacity required. Mission-specific systems primarily assign highly creative roles to the senior headquarters, with selective-control systems both needing more overall capacity and having more potential for automation of those functions they perform. Objective-oriented systems (which require somewhat more capacity) can be more automated. In particular, the problem-solving system in which detailed guidelines and planning for logistics and other support are relatively simple to automate can be managed at the higher levels. Interventionist systems need the most capacity, but are also the easiest to automate because they rely more on prior training and are designed to generate prepackaged, good-enough, or suboptimal solutions that can be implemented successfully. Cyclic headquarters are designed to do the same work as interventionist (issue orders) but perform each task less often, which reduces their need for overall capacity.

Note, however, that the increased responsibility and authority delegated to lower units in mission-oriented structures also means that these units must have (a) greater information, knowledge, and situational understanding, and (b) more capacity to collaborate and synchronize their actions.

Spectrum of C2 Organization Options

As Figure 66 indicates, a range of C2 organizational options is available in the Information Age. The technical capability exists to support every option from fully centralized to fully decentralized (self-synchronization). The case of no organization at all has been disregarded since it implies no structure, functional specialization, or organizational capacity. Hence, it implies a leaderless mass not connected by commander's intent, making cooperation a random event. The ideal C2 organization for Information Age Warfare remains unproven, but is hypothesized to be collaborative and decentralized C2 with the complexity of the mission, the need to cooperate with others (coalitions, non-governmental actors, etc.), the quality of the supporting information technologies, the need for specialized functions such as logistics and time coordination, the quality of the units, and the degree to which common doctrine, tactics, and procedures are available, all impacting the best choice. Serious research, including experimentation, will be needed to resolve this issue. This may be the single most important arena where research is necessary. Old structures will be seriously depleted unless new ones are shown to be superior.

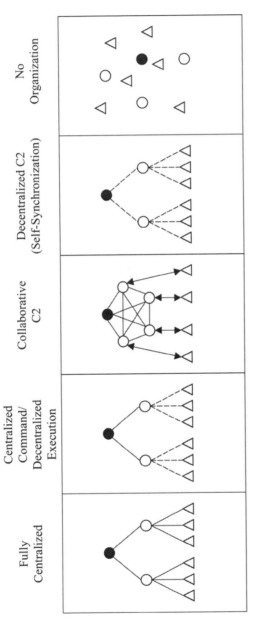

Figure 66. Spectrum of C2 Organization Options

The fact that all of these organizational types remain relevant is demonstrated in Figure 67. Each of these ideal types, except no organization, have demonstrable benefits as well as known costs. At least in theory, decentralized C2, or self-synchronization, holds the greatest promise. We hypothesize, therefore, that Information Age organizational innovation should move in that direction. At the same time, collaborative C2, which makes less demand on the quality of the units available and may be a better match for the existing force structures, also appears to be an attractive target. Note, moreover, that the key issues appear to be within our control—generating effective and efficient collaboration tools and training.

Type	Fully Centralized	Centralized Command/ Decentralized Execution	Collaborative C2	Decentralized C2 (Self-Synchronization)	No Organization
Example	72-hour ATO	Desert Storm	Bosnia & Kosovo	Submarine Operations Guerrilla Operations SOF	Rout or Chaotic
Benefits	Optimum Use of Assets	•Near Optimum Resource Allocation •Encourages Initiative	•Higher Quality Decision Making •Units Tightly Coupled •Robust	•Low Overhead •Responsive to Local Situation Changes	Unpredictable to Adversary
Costs	Enormous Overhead/ Brittle	Potential for Mutual Interference or Missed Opportunities	•Can Be Slow to Respond •Requires Collaborative Tools and Cooperability	Highly Professional Quasi-Autonomous Units Required	•Synergy Accidental •Mutual Interference Likely

Figure 67. Information Age C2 Organizations

Organizational progress can be expected to be a slow process, but can also be the focus of important and exciting exploration, research, and experimentation. Programs designed to make progress in this area must be a top priority.

---

[1]Col. John R. Boyd, USAF, *Patterns of Conflict* (Unpublished Lecture, 1977). Col. John R. Boyd, USAF, "A Discourse on Winning and Losing." A collection of unpublished briefings and essays (Maxwell AFB, AL: Air University Library, 1976-1992), http://www.belisarius.com/modern_business_strategy/boyd/essence/eowl_frameset.htm, January 1996.

[2]Vadm Arthur K. Cebrowski, USN, and John J. Gartska, "Network Centric Warfare: Its Origin and Future," *Proceedings of the Naval Institute* 124:1 (January, 1998), pp. 28-35.

[3]*Headquarters Effectiveness Program Summary Task 002* (McLean, VA: Defense Systems, Inc., September 1983).

CHAPTER 8

What Is Collaboration?

Understanding Collaboration in a Military Context

Collaboration, as used here, involves actors actively sharing data, information, knowledge, perceptions (awareness of facts or factors, understandings of situations, etc.), or concepts when they are working together toward a common purpose and how they might achieve that purpose efficiently or effectively.

Note, first, what collaboration is not. When information systems passively (without current, conscious human intent) share data, information, or knowledge (for example doctrinal publications) or make it available to a variety of users, no collaboration has taken place. These are simple cases of sharing. Moreover, exchanges that are not related to a common purpose should be excluded. For example, routine reports on unit status or spot reports on enemy activity are normally only loosely coupled to the tasks, missions, or objectives of the organization and are shared passively, not actively. Similarly, routine briefings, such as the "5 o'clock follies" in many command centers, are not collaborative events unless the participants take advantage of them to interact to resolve particular issues.

Collaboration, then, requires active communication as part of working together. The classic military example is collaborative planning, where actors with different functional and geographic areas of responsibility focus their attention on achieving assigned missions. Their goals are to create a common (shared) understanding of the situation; take advantage of their differential knowledge, expertise, information, and capabilities; and organize the activities they control in time and space such that they will (a) avoid mutual interference and (b) have a synergistic effect. In other words, they want to plan so their actions will be synchronized. Of course, collaboration may well extend into an integrated process of execution/replanning as the mission is pursued.

Integrated product teams are essentially organizational forms designed to encourage (or ensure) collaboration takes place. They were created under the theory that complex problems often require functionally different expertise. They assume that the costs of the collaboration (whether time or resources) will more than be recovered by the higher quality of the results, which blend the knowledge available from the different sources. In some cases they are also seen as more rapid, particularly when they replace serial processes where each group waited for another to finish before they could begin, or processes that shut down while people rested. In that sense, military command centers, which have employed shifts over time and used overlapping duty hours to hand off their knowledge and situational awareness for decades, were pioneers in collaboration. However, most of that collaboration historically took place within functional areas.

Finally, inherent in the idea of collaboration in a military context is the notion that a mission will be accomplished. When the collaboration is used to ensure more efficient mission accomplishment, the appropriate metrics are Measures of Performance (MOP) that show how the same level of effectiveness can be accomplished with fewer resources or higher levels achieved with the same level of resources. These metrics often focus on residual force levels or capacity after mission accomplishment, but can also look at levels or rates of force expenditure during mission accomplishment. When the focus is on mission accomplishment itself, the appropriate metrics are Measures of Effectiveness (MOE), and may also extend to Measures of Force Effectiveness (MOFE), or Measures of Policy Effectiveness (MOPE).

How Can Collaboration Differ?

The first key to understanding a concept is to define it clearly, the second is to describe it well. Collaboration has a number of different dimensions, each of which can vary. These include media, time required, continuity, breadth, content richness, domain, structure, participant roles, and the linkages across which it takes place. Small wonder, then, that scholars have trouble measuring collaboration and its impact. This multidimensional concept must be decomposed and the variety of its significant dimensions must be controlled in order for researchers to observe and measure its quality and its impact.

Most obviously, collaboration varies by medium. Face-to-face is the standard against which all others are measured. Video teleconferencing is the most elaborate alternative and has been used by senior U.S. commanders in planning and executing complex operations such as Haiti. White boards and other technologies that allow actors to look at the same images have also become widely available and are used increasingly. Not only Microsoft PowerPoint, but other types of shared images (maps, overlays, etc.) are now readily available. Voice technologies have long been a standard on the battlefield and have proven robust. Teletypes remain available in some command centers, though they have largely been supplanted by computer technologies that allow more immediate exchange of written messages, such as e-mail. In some command centers and across echelons of some commands, e-mail has become the dominant medium for collaboration. Computer technologies also allow common use of data and databases to support the collaboration process.

The time required for a given medium to enable collaboration can also vary. As communications technologies continue to mature and interoperability problems are resolved across warfare arenas and functional specializations, this factor will become less of a constraint on the collaboration process. However, collaborative processes consume time—the actors have to communicate with one another. They also engage in a variety of behaviors inherent in the collaboration process—exchanging information, establishing agendas and priorities, negotiating about the process and the common ground they will agree on when addressing the problem, positing alternative approaches and solutions, and so forth. All these require time.

Collaboration can also differ in terms of *continuity,* or whether the process is synchronous or asynchronous. When distributed headquarters are working in different time zones or the task is such that one actor is distracted or unavailable, collaboration tools that do not require continuous participation (such as e-mail) may be preferable. However, they have some impact on the quality of the interaction. Whether that is an improvement (everyone is working on their prime time, actors have a chance to examine inputs and give them thought before responding) or a decrement (lack of timely inquiry and response, delay, absence of dialogue or free wheeling discussion) is not well understood. In all likelihood, the impact of continuity and the circumstances under which it is desirable will require applied research.

The breadth of collaboration is also important. This reflects who participates, including the question of whether all the relevant types of expertise are available during the collaborative process. Sheer numbers also matter. All other things being equal, more people will require more time to establish common ground and to generate consensus on what is to be done as well as how to go about it.

The richness of the content must also be recognized as a dimension in collaboration. At a very basic level, individuals may be working together by simply sharing information and data. Genuine collaboration, however, requires that they be dealing at the conceptual level by pooling their knowledge and/or exploring their understandings of the situation. Discussions that seek agreement on facts are not as rich as those that seek to place those facts into context, identify the patterns within them that help the actors to correctly classify the situation and understand its significance for them, examine ways to influence that situation, and project the alternative futures that may arise from it. Most instances of collaboration are, therefore, in both the cognitive and information domains. While the creative part of the process takes place in the brains of the individuals involved, the actual exchange of ideas requires the use of the information domain.

Collaboration processes can also differ in *structure*. This actually implies several possible differences. First, the authority structure can vary. Pure peer groups will operate very differently than hierarchical groups in which leaders are apparent. Groups can also differ in a role when the members are functional specialists or generalists for the problem at hand. Structure also includes the communication pattern—whether the members of the group are multiconnected or connected by some other pattern. Research by the Soviets has shown that different dynamics occur in hierarchical communication, wheels and spokes, simple stars, and multiconnected systems.[1] Finally, structures also differ in terms of task organization. Some collaboration is between individuals with different functional roles who are seeking to coordinate their activities, others are conducted between individuals who share functional responsibilities. Such groups may also be temporary (brought together only for a time to accomplish a specific task or set of tasks) or permanent.

The roles of the actors, in ways other than authority relationships, can also differ. Specialists and generalists play different roles, as do those who are integrators and facilitators in the team. These roles, in turn, help to determine the types of boundaries spanned. These are most often functional boundaries, but in C4ISR they may also be boundaries between echelons of command, across geography (spatial boundaries), or over time (when current operations are blended with future plans).

Regardless of the type of collaboration, information technologies are only enablers. In many military situations collaboration is difficult or impossible unless specialized technologies are available. However, whether collaboration occurs at all, and the quality of the collaboration is determined by a number of external factors, including leadership (is collaboration made a priority, does the commander set a tone of interaction, etc.), organization, doctrine, training, experience, perceived time available, and the established TTP (tactics, techniques, and procedures) of the force.

Collaboration in the Information Domain: State of the Practice

Traditional collaboration in the information domain has extended to little more than data sharing in the terms used in this volume. Data was often processed locally or at very high levels and not really shared across echelons or functional arenas. Each command center acted as a sink for both data and information, soaking up all it could find and expending major effort to integrate it and come up with a rich understanding of the military situation. The lack of automated data processing capability and the limited band width available within and across command centers encouraged functional specialization throughout the system. The Napoleonic staff structure, designed to decompose the work of command centers, dominated organizational thinking, creating stovepipes both within and across command centers. Everything was designed to distill essences and present them to the commanders and key staff members. Drill down capability, recognized as important at all levels, was organized into these same relatively isolated functional areas. While efforts were made to coordinate both up and down the chain of command and across functional areas, these efforts were heavily restricted by the communications technologies available and also often carried on within functional stovepipes.

This traditional system meant that most collaboration took place in the form of C4ISR products: briefings, reports, displays, plans, orders, etc. These products were heavily formatted according to doctrine and agreed TTPs. This made them familiar and relatively easy to use. However, they also lacked richness— data with differing latencies were mixed together, the uncertainty underlying presentations was not displayed and often known only to those who prepared the products. Assumptions (templates when adversary unit locations were only partially known, rates of movement assigned to friendly and adversary forces, etc.) were seldom made explicit.

This austere collaboration capability was made worse by interoperability problems. The intelligence function had, for security reasons, independent communications systems. The logistic functions, because they involved a great deal of traffic, developed another independent set of communications. Fires were controlled on systems that were also independent of the command nets, though these two systems could usually be brought together in an emergency. However, controllers for close air support were traditionally on a different system from those responsible for ground fire. In many cases commanders would literally call together their subordinate commanders and/or key staff to collaborate because there was no other way to ensure a rich common understanding of the mission, commanders intent, and the selected course of action.

Traditional C2, because of weak information sharing, was often a quest to ensure that mutual interference in the battlespace was avoided. For example, in a series of division-level U.S. Army exercises in the 1980s, a primary problem turned out to be the coordination of road use in the rear areas. When these problems were avoided, unit performance was greatly improved. Similarly, when collaboration is heavily constrained, the creativity of commanders at all levels is restricted. This almost guarantees that the only synergy that occurs is that already recognized in doctrine or TTP.

Collaboration in the Information Domain: State of the Possible

When collaboration in the information domain is enriched, considerable improvement can be expected. First, the sharing of data greatly improves the likelihood of developing a common (shared) picture of the battlespace. When data is pooled from sensors, the quality of the underlying database can be expected to improve. That same database will also be more up to date—the delay inherent in one sitting on a data item, placing it into a product, and disseminating that product all but disappears. In essence, the fusion of information which greatly enhances its richness or quality is significantly improved by sharing data.

Second, by sharing information more rapidly a similar value-generating effect occurs—more command centers are aware of more information sooner. This has potential synergistic impacts. The information item is seen from multiple perspectives—for example, its intelligence, operations, and logistics implications can be recognized sooner. Similarly, reviewing the data from multiple perspectives increases the likelihood of anomaly detection. This decreases false alarms and guards against bad data. This is very important because even a little bad data goes a long way to degrading one's information position. Working in a highly uncertain environment with adversaries who are attempting to conceal their activities and deceive the friendly C4ISR system makes anomaly detection a crucial tool in maintaining high quality situation awareness. Finally, the more rapid dissemination of information by means of preset automated data sharing also allows for more rapid integration of new data into battlespace awareness. In the Information Age, speed of command will often be crucial.

Finally, Information Age systems also allow for better availability of prior knowledge. Military forces, particularly technologically sophisticated ones, depend on the doctrine, training, and skills of their personnel. However, not all forces are fully up to speed in all areas all the time. Forces train for a set of operating environments, with an expected set of coalition partners, and specific classes of adversaries, as well as with particular types of equipment. The global responsibilities of the U.S. military, however, virtually guarantee that some unfamiliar locations, adversaries, equipment, or coalition partners will be encountered. An Information Age military will, however, have enormous reach-back capability to access knowledge and examine it both individually and collectively. Access to databases (plans and detailed maps of urban environments, order of battle data for unanticipated coalition partners and adversaries), manuals (field repairs for specialized equipment or foreign equipment used in the theater), information sets (symptoms for local diseases or biological weapons), and knowledge (local customs, adversary doctrine, profiles of enemy leaders) all will enable improved operational effectiveness.

However, this improved sharing of information does not come without costs. These costs will primarily be in the form of greater demands for bandwidth to deliver the shared information and an increased need for computational power (either in the rear or forward) to organize and present it. The human factor problem of accepting what comes from a computer as real and failing to understand the uncertainty inherent in that computer product is an important issue and must be addressed both in the training of users and in the design of information systems and representations.

Perhaps most important, sharing information in the battlespace will make demands on the time and attention of commanders and key staff members who are already heavily burdened (physically and cognitively). These individuals will also be tired and under stress. Early work with computers inside armored vehicles has shown that displays can distract key personnel from their immediate warfighting tasks. Hence, human factors will be a crucial element in designing effective ways to share information.

Collaboration in the Cognitive Domain

All collaboration passes through the information domain, even when face-to-face, collaborators send information (voice, facial expressions) to their partners. However, collaboration—sharing in order to work together toward a common purpose—actually occurs in the cognitive domain as the partners interact and develop awareness, knowledge, understanding, and concepts that would not have emerged without these exchanges.

Clearly collaboration requires communication. While this is often direct, it can certainly be asynchronous. For example, academic authors have long collaborated by exchanging written drafts, with episodic meetings and discussions. More recently, e-mail has made this process faster and simpler. However, the quality of the interaction can vary greatly, depending on whether the collaborators share a common language, background, and culture (national and organizational), the level of engagement of the participants (are they serious, do they accept the goal), their confidence in the collaboration medium (including their ability to use it when technical capability is required), and previous opportunities to work together.

The potential benefits of cognitive collaboration are enormous. A better understanding of the military situation and the factors that are driving it are the most obvious benefits and correspond to a common understanding of the problem in the civilian arena. The opportunity to improve planning through collaboration is also enormous. Involving both those responsible for conducting an operation and those responsible for supporting it enables the development of a much richer plan as well as the achievement of greater insights into the contingencies that can be expected. Collaborative decisionmaking can be expected to generate better choices, particularly when complex problems are being addressed. Finally, collaboration will improve the linkage between planning and execution. As these two functions merge, effective collaboration will provide greater organizational agility—the capacity to react more effectively in a rapidly changing operating environment.

There is one potential drawback that should be anticipated when collaboration is used—a loss of speed in the C4ISR process. Research into small group dynamics, decisionmaking under stress, crisis decisionmaking, and coalition C4ISR indicates that collaboration slows decisionmaking.[2] Hence, collaboration tools need to be designed with this pitfall in mind. At a minimum, training in the use of a collaborative environment and tools and the development of new processes that are designed to work in a collaborative environment will be essential if this and other potential problems are to be minimized. Increased contingency planning to take advantage of the richer interaction and deeper understanding of the problem is also needed so that novel decisions in complex situations can be reduced.

Measuring Collaboration

Learning how to use collaboration effectively will require a considerable amount of experimentation, which requires the ability to measure the nature and characteristics of the collaborative environment and processes being tried. Measuring collaboration is a challenge primarily because of the many dimensions along which it varies. While collaboration is not a goal in itself within command and control, the C4ISR analytic community needs to help design and improve collaboration tools and to understand how collaboration, C2, and mission accomplishment are related. Like better information, collaboration is a tool designed to help decisionmaking, planning, and force synchronization. The ultimate payoff is, therefore, in effective and efficient actions that lead to mission accomplishment. There is no correct level of collaboration in the abstract. The focus of research should be to identify those forms and levels of collaboration that pay off in military operations.

This implies that collaboration researchers need to be constantly aware of the context in which collaboration occurs—what kinds of groups, engaged in what types of tasks, benefited in what ways, from which types of collaboration, supported by what tools. In many cases, the sheer complexity of the environment and the number of ways collaboration can vary will make it impossible to measure its impact cleanly. However, it should be possible to correctly characterize the collaboration tools present in a given case and to accumulate research results across cases in a multidimensional space that describe collaboration applications.

Research teams will also have to collect data on the degree of collaboration that takes place—frequency of interaction, number of participants, and so forth. A standard set of metrics for this is possible, though controlling for the opportunities to collaborate will always be a challenge. Observers can begin by recognizing the absence of collaboration. *Zero collaboration* can be defined as the absence of working together toward a common goal, regardless of whether some information sharing occurs. Failure to actively share in the cognitive domain (concepts, understandings, and knowledge) would also mean that no collaboration had taken place, even if the participants shared a common goal.

To take a simple example, a submarine or special forces team that is assigned a mission and then goes silent while they carry it out cannot collaborate with other senior headquarters or other units, but they can self-synchronize their actions if they are able to maintain an awareness of the situation, even though they may be receiving new information about the situation. In a more complicated case, two organizations reporting through different chains of command and assigned radically different missions may not be able to collaborate because they do not share a common purpose. For instance, an attack asset may destroy an adversary communications system in order to carry out its mission to disrupt enemy communications while an information operations asset may be intercepting traffic from that system in order to meet its collection requirements and give the field commander an information advantage. It can be anticipated that internal conflicts such as this will be more likely to be uncovered and fixed as attempts are made to increase collaboration throughout the force.

Maximum collaboration, on the other hand, can only occur when certain specific capabilities exist. Given that two or more actors are seen to be sharing at the conceptual level and working together toward a common purpose, their collaboration can be seen as maximized if it is:

- *Inclusive*:
    - all the relevant actors are involved; and
    - the collaboration cuts across organizational, functional, spatial, and temporal boundaries, including echelons of command;
- *Multiconnected* (every actor has access to all other actors);
- *Unrestricted communication* (between the collaborators);
- *Participatory* (all relevant actors are engaged in the process);
- *Continuous* (actors are engaged without disruption);
- *Simultaneous* (synchronous);
- *Media-rich* (face-to-face, with shared images, information, and data);
- *Domain-rich* (involves both the cognitive and the information domains); and
- *Content-rich* (involves data, information, knowledge, and understandings).

From a research perspective, each collaboration situation (experiment, exercise, etc.) can be characterized both in terms of the kinds of collaboration that are possible (for example, face-to-face is not universally available in distributed command centers) and what actually takes place (for example, continuous collaboration is enabled, but the actors only collaborate 6 hours per day).

Maximum collaboration is, however, only possible in a context that is appropriate in that it both motivates the actors and enables them to cooperate. Recent research on collaboration in military contexts has shown that there are structural and situational impediments to success.[3]

First, the collaborators must be in agreement about the importance and legitimacy of the goal being pursued. This does not mean that they will have complete or precise agreement on the goal or purpose. Specification of the goal and reaching consensus on what it really is are often topics of collaboration. However, unless the actors see the goal as legitimate and important, they are not motivated to work together or to make the investments (temporal, informational, mental, or physical) necessary for success. For similar reasons, the actors must also have at least a general common understanding of the purpose or goal. Without this, the dialogue cannot be joined. Given broad agreement, the parties can have meaningful discussions.

Second, the collaborators need to be able to communicate with one another. This implies that they have some common language about the problem space. Here, again, the group can be expected to develop a more specialized language about the particular problem when they collaborate. However, unless they can describe the problem space in a way they all understand, they will not be able to reach consensus on how they can proceed. In addition, effective communication implies that the collaborators have both competence in using the collaboration technology and confidence in the technology itself. When the collaboration process is disrupted by poor human factors (lack of training in the use of the environment or tools or a mistrust of those tools), the individuals involved are not likely to be highly motivated and their communications are likely to be disjointed and potentially dysfunctional.

Maximum collaboration, and the success of the collaboration that does occur, also depends on the participants' knowledge and understanding of one another. This implies that the participants are all familiar with one another's backgrounds, training, and cultures (both national and organizational). When this precondition is not met, most groups will find it necessary to invest some time in introductions and discussion of the various perspectives within the group. In addition, the roles of the participants need to be well understood within the group. This includes knowing who the leaders are, what representational roles are present (organizational, disciplinary, etc.), specializations within the group, and so forth. Only when these conditions are met does the group find it easy to collaborate effectively.

---

[1]Monograph by V.V. Druzhinin "Concept, Algorithm, Decision (A Soviet View)" (Moscow: Translated and published under auspices of USAF, USGPO, Volume 6 of "Soviet Military Thought," Series Stock # 0870-00344, 1972).

[2]David S. Alberts and Richard E. Hayes, *Command Arrangements for Peace Operations* (Washington, DC: National Defense University Press, May 1995).

[3]Julia Loughran and Marcy Stahl, "The DICE Experiment: Creating and Evaluating a Web-based Collaboration Environment for Interagency Training" briefing (Vienna, VA: ThoughtLink, Inc., May 2000), http://www.thoughtlink.com/publications/TLI-DICE99Abstract.htm

CHAPTER 9

Synchronization

Focus

The previous section covered collaboration enabled by improved networking and quality of information, its potential role in C2 processes, and its importance as a means of improving shared awareness and speed of decisionmaking in order to rapidly synchronize forces and keep pace with the dynamics of modern military operations.

This chapter begins by defining the concept of synchronization of forces in terms of its relationship to the C2 process, its importance to military operations, challenges that must be addressed in achieving it, and possible means of meeting these challenges through increased networking and new C2 concepts. We then put forth hypotheses that need to be examined regarding the means of achieving synchronization, as well as its impact on force effectiveness and operational outcomes, and identify key attributes of synchronization that need to be measured and the metrics necessary to do so. This chapter concludes with the description of experiments that could be conducted to investigate the validity of these hypotheses.

What Is Synchronization?

Synchronization is defined by Webster quite eloquently as "the purposeful arrangement of things in time and space."[1] In a military context, synchronization can be thought of as an output characteristic of the C2 processes that arrange and continually adapt the relationships of actions (including moving and tasking forces) in time and space in order to achieve the established objective(s). This characterization of synchronization implies some important properties worth noting.

First, synchronization occurs in the physical domain. It involves the transformation of ideas and concepts in the heads of commanders, staff planners, and troops into real world events through the processing and transmission of information. It therefore requires fusing the cognitive, information, and physical domains. In fact, as the speed of decisionmaking and information flows associated with the C2 process increase, the dynamics associated with the force elements in the physical domain will define the limits of overall synchronization. Even as force elements are redesigned for greater speed, there will always be some such limit because they cannot move at the speed of thought or information.

Second, achieving the necessary degree of synchronization will require a C2 organizational concept with a level of centralization or decentralization that provides the appropriate degree of guidance and flexibility for the type of environment, mission, troops, and information support capabilities being considered.

Third, synchronization often involves both vertical and horizontal harmonization. It requires vertical harmonization over multiple echelons of the organization and aggregation/disaggregation of activities that are of interest at these different echelons in order to ensure that actions at the lowest tactical levels are consistent with higher level operational and strategic goals. It requires horizontal harmonization across multiple dimensions of the C2 process, including those associated with different organizations, functional areas, types of force, and portions of the operational space.

Although this chapter will discuss how such properties can be achieved through the selection of an appropriate C2 concept, we must begin with a discussion of why synchronization is becoming increasingly important to the success of military operations and why, at the same time, it is becoming more difficult to achieve.

Why Is Synchronization Important?

Synchronization has been a fundamental concept in warfare throughout history. Setting aside conflicts involving the animal kingdom, the seeds of strategies related to synchronization can be seen in the skills developed for hand-to-hand combat between two adversaries (manifested today in sports such as wrestling, boxing, and other martial arts), where the speed, sequence, and timing of offensive and defensive moves relative to those of an opponent were often the key to victory. While warfare involving multiple combatants is more complex (football and soccer become more apt analogies) and the degree of complexity has grown over the years, the ability to synchronize various aspects of operations has continued to be an important, and in many cases the decisive, factor. In fact, synchronization can contribute to improved force effectiveness and efficiency and increase the likelihood of successful operational outcome in several ways that are consistent with the Principles of Warfare. These are summarized below.

Shaping the Battlespace

The key to gaining a decisive advantage in warfare is to capitalize on one's own strengths while exploiting the weaknesses of adversaries. This means proactively orchestrating events in order to shape the course of the battle so that engagements take place on terms that are most favorable to friendly forces and least favorable to enemy forces. This includes controlling the time and place of engagements to maintain momentum in a manner that is matched to the dynamics of the friendly forces while exploiting or disrupting the cycle(s) of enemy activity. It also includes coordinating active measures with deceptive measures intended to cause an adversary to commit his forces in such a way that they become vulnerable to friendly forces prepared to exploit such opportunities.

Classic examples abound. Stonewall Jackson's famous campaigns in the Shenandoah Valley were based on superior intelligence (reports of Union movements from southern sympathizers), a rich appreciation of the terrain (knowledge of key passes and routes), superior speed of movement (his famous "foot cavalry"), and the ability to keep Union forces from knowing about his movements. As a result, the Union forces were spread thin, trying to cover all of Jackson's possible avenues of advance, and could be fought piecemeal. Jackson was therefore able to inflict a series of defeats while pinning down forces that were, numerically, far superior.[2]

The importance of deception and effective maneuver was also demonstrated by the Japanese in the Battle of Leyte Gulf during World War II. Lacking the force necessary to directly penetrate American defenses and disrupt the invasion force moving into the Philippines, the Japanese Admiral divided his fleet. One element deliberately showed itself and was able to draw off a major portion of the American naval force under Admiral Halsey, thus exploiting his eagerness to destroy the remaining Japanese carriers. A second Japanese element was then able to attack the lightly escorted amphibious force, which included several smaller escort carriers. This tactic nearly worked and ultimately thwarted only the courage and tenacity of the personnel fighting the escort carriers and accompanying destroyers.

Shaping the battlespace is a time-honored tradition, but the Information Age makes it possible to do so in new ways. Perhaps the best recent examples were the U.S.-led coalition's large scale deception operations during *Desert Shield* that were designed to shape the Iraqi posture. Major elements of that program included (a) allowing broad press access to USMC landing exercises that confirmed Iraqi expectations of an amphibious assault and therefore pinned major Iraqi forces down along the coast, well away from the true attack area; (b) heavy air attacks that blinded Iraqi forces and reduced their mobility and communications capacity, making it impossible for them to effectively see the preparations for the "left hook" or maneuver to meet it once it became apparent; and (c) the prepositioning of major forces in front of an initial bluff attack by heavy forces up a major wadi where the Iraqi's expected a major assault.

Focusing Effects

Another long-standing tactic is to rapidly mass ground forces or focus long-range fires to gain a local advantage that can be further exploited before the enemy can react. For example, the Soviet concept of correlation of forces required synchronization to ensure that the concentration of forces at key points along the front would be sufficiently high to guarantee the breakthrough and positioning of second echelon forces, which would arrive and exploit the opportunity to penetrate the opponent's rear before the breach could be closed. This Soviet concept was a direct outgrowth of the German *blitzkrieg*, which they had experienced devastating early in World War II.

In a very different warfighting arena, guerrilla warfare focuses effects as a primary concept. The typical guerrilla objective is to use small initiatives (destruction of bridges, ambushing supply convoys, raids on isolated elements, mine laying, etc.) that pin down large forces and demonstrate the guerrillas' commitment to achieving their objectives. The goal is twofold: to persuade the conventional force that it cannot win and to influence the government (through high casualties and the threat of an endless, bloody campaign), so that it will either withdraw that force or grant autonomy rather than continue to pay the price. Hence, the effect is both far distant from the actual battlespace and also on a completely different level from the fighting.

Synergy

Finally, the ability to synchronize the application of different types of force elements permits them to be used in a synergistic manner. For example, the combined arms doctrine developed by U.S. and Soviet forces calls for the use of armor, infantry, artillery, air support, and air defense in a coordinated manner in order to capitalize on the strengths of each component while minimizing exposure of friendly forces.

The weapons, tactics, and techniques of modern air strikes are also a classic case of synergy. The attacking force is made up of specialized elements: electronic surveillance and jamming aircraft to pinpoint and reduce the effectiveness of radars and air defenses; overhead space assets that provide important sensor data; attack aircraft with specialized weapons (for example HARM missiles designed to home in on and kill air defense radars); perhaps stealth aircraft designed to strike the most heavily defended targets or key elements of the air defense system; aircraft assigned to destroy adversary fighters on the ground or crater runways so they cannot come up and participate in the defense; fighters to engage and destroy interceptors; perhaps long-range stand-off weapons that minimize the risk to platforms; and attack aircraft armed with precision munitions: all coordinated by airborne platforms such as AWACS. The enormous complexity of these enterprises is precisely the kind of opportunity created by increased capabilities in the information domain.

The simple, bloody logic of guerrilla warfare and terrorism also illustrates the use of synergy. Raids, ambushes, and attacks on isolated forces are often linked to ambushes of the relief force. Terrorist organizations have learned to set off one bomb while positioning and timing a second so that it will hurt the security and medical personnel responding to the initial casualties.

As noted above, there are numerous historical examples that illustrate the importance of synchronization, and it can be expected to become even more important as we ponder warfare in the 21st century. Already apparent today are many contributing factors whose impact can be expected to grow in the future. For example, there is increasing pressure for low casualties and collateral damage that can only be achieved through more precise application of force.

Why It Is Becoming More Difficult to Achieve and Maintain Synchronization in Military Operations

At the same time that synchronization is becoming more important in military operations, achieving synchronization is becoming more challenging for a number of reasons. These include increasing complexity, growing heterogeneity, and a faster pace of events.

Increasing Complexity

There have always been large numbers of entities with varying degrees of freedom in military operations. However, today we see an ever increasing desire for more precision and the increasing need for battlefield entities to work together. Furthermore, because of the growing lethality of the battlefield due to improvements in both sensors and weapons, there is also a trend toward distributed operations with dispersed forces who must operate in concert to control the battlespace. The resultant need for closer coupling and precise effects has resulted in increased complexity of operations.

Growing Heterogeneity

Coordinating across multiple echelons and organizational entities with different cultures, processes, perceptions, and response cycles has been a consideration in many past conflicts. However, the central role of coalition warfare operations in U.S. national security strategy requires that we be prepared to militarily interoperate with a host of potential allies to a degree unheard of before. The emergence of operations other than war demands that we be able to interoperate with non-government organizations as well. Because of uncertainty regarding the threat and type of operation, it will be difficult to rationalize beforehand the many differences that must be overcome to achieve the level of interoperability necessary to achieve a high degree of synchronization in coalition operations. The sheer variety in the nature of the organizations (other than U.S. Government, allies, other coalition partners, NGOs, international organizations) combine to make coalition operations, particularly OOTW operations, more challenging.

Faster Pace of Events

Improvements in sensors promise to help U.S. forces cope with the increased pace of events in the modern battlespace. However, in order to truly capitalize on the information they provide and deal with the residual uncertainties that are inevitable, C2 processes must be extremely adaptive and the associated synchronization capability very agile. Depending upon the size, complexity, and dynamics of the operation, traditional centralized C2 processes are likely to be challenged and perhaps give way to other forms of organization and command approaches.

Research sponsored by the Army Research Institute has shown, for example, that U.S. Army divisions, which were tasked by doctrine in 1988 to produce plans that looked 72 hours into the future, were, in fact, during command post exercises, actually changing those plans every 9 hours.[3] This research proved insightful. When *Desert Storm* kicked off, divisions (U.S. and coalition) found that the pace of events far outstripped their ability to plan in the ways they had studied. Instead, they found themselves engaged in "command and control on the fly" as they struggled to keep their forces coordinated and their activities synchronized. Improved communications and tools for better information sharing and collaborative planning will help commanders deal with the increasing pace of battle in the future. Joint and Service experimentation will perhaps discover and refine adaptive planning and C2 approaches and processes.

Taken together, the growing complexity, heterogeneity, and pace of the battlespace greatly compound the problem of achieving and maintaining synchronization. Clearly, new approaches must be explored.

How Does Networking Enable Synchronization?

Earlier discussion focused on how an integrated information infrastructure, including increased networking, could help transform the C2 process from one that involves sequential periodic processes and limited interactions among largely isolated communities to one characterized by highly parallel, continuous processes that are more collaborative and integrated vertically across echelons and horizontally across disparate functional areas. As indicated in Figure 68, this transformation is enabled by the simultaneous improvements in richness, reach, and richness of reach promised by increased networking. Furthermore, the factors that facilitate new C2 concepts are the very factors that permit the associated C2 processes to achieve higher degrees of synchronization. They include:

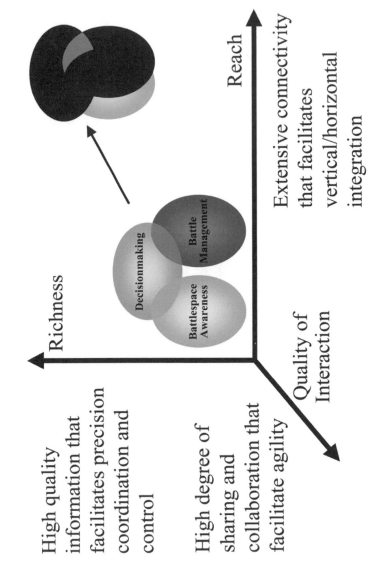

Figure 68. How Does Networking Enable Synchronization?

- *Richness of Information*: The high quality information (e.g., location, accuracy, timeliness, classification) facilitates precision control of, or high degree of, coordination among force elements.

- *Reach*: All relevant elements across the spectrum of echelons and functional areas can participate dynamically through improved networking.

- *Quality of Interaction*: A high degree of information sharing and collaboration permit dispersed elements to rapidly adjust plans, schedules, and actions in accordance with changes in the situation.

The bottom line is that the potential exists to achieve greater precision and increased synchronization across a broad range of force elements and agility (adjusting to changes in the operational situation in a timely manner).

What Are the Various Means That Can Be Used to Achieve Synchronization?

There are a wide variety of means for achieving synchronization. These vary in the degree to which force elements must be prepared before the operation, the degree of centralization/decentralization of the C2 process, and the degree of relevant information sharing and collaboration. The following are brief descriptions and important examples along the synchronization spectrum.

Shared Prior Knowledge

The traditional means of achieving synchronization is through the development and promulgation of doctrine, tactics, and procedures. Extensive education and training can be used to create a culture of teamwork based on common understanding of the mission, means of achieving the mission, and language for applying these means. U.S. Special Operations Forces have mastered the art of extensive training, detailed planning (including contingencies), mission rehearsal, and aggressive execution.

Highly Centralized Command and Control

Command and control can be fully centralized so that not only is all planning and scheduling done centrally, but detailed direction to the forces is also provided by a central authority. This is generally practical only for small operations with a relatively stable environment. However, the USAF traditional Air Tasking Order is an excellent example of a highly centralized, effective form of command and control.

Centralized Command and Decentralized Control

More often top-level planning and scheduling is conducted centrally and subsequent decisions associated with the details of execution are decentralized. This is the model underlying both U.S. Army and U.S. Navy command and control as well as a principle built into U.S. Joint and NATO doctrines.

Collaborative C2

In this case, C2 nodes up and down the chain are collaborating with each other and the forces to continually adjust plans, schedules, and decisions related to execution as important aspects of the situation change. Perhaps the best extant example is Israeli command and control practice. However the collaborative planning process used by U.S. Special Forces is also a very real example.

Self-Synchronization

One example of this type of highly decentralized C2 calls for lower-level decisionmakers to be guided only by their training, understanding of the commander's intent, and their awareness of the situation in relevant portions of the battlespace. In some variants of this concept there is a provision for management by exception (i.e., the commander can negate lower-level decisions on an exception basis). Submarine forces often operate this way in order to avoid communications that might give away the locations or missions.

What Is the Role of Planning in Synchronization?

Since planning and scheduling are usually the primary means associated with achieving synchronization, it is worth examining the variations in the types of plans associated with the different means. For the highly centralized C2 of large operations, plan-driven C2 is most often used. Because these plans tend to be inflexible, they are most appropriate in situations where uncertainty is low and the situation is fairly stable. However, as is often the case, because of the difficulty in accurately predicting how combat situations will unfold, plans do not often survive first contact with the enemy. The plans used by Egypt in the 1973 war with the Israelis are a prime example; they did not provide sufficient flexibility to deal with the Israeli response to Egypt's initial attack. Indeed, their goal was to achieve initial success and then halt to rearm, resupply, and reinforce. The Israeli's were able to exploit this scheduled break in Egyptian operations to regain the initiative.

On the other hand, more general plans that convey intent can be used as a means of empowering forces and providing flexibility to accommodate unexpected changes in the situation. Admiral Nelson employed a more flexible concept at Trafalgar: an initial plan was used to engage the Spanish fleet while the training and shared understanding of Nelson's concept for battle permitted his forces to break through and exploit the resulting opportunities.

This variation in plan flexibility is summarized in Figure 69. Flexibility can be achieved by permitting the details of the plan to evolve along with the situation, as in the case of collaborative C2, or by reducing the level of detail provided (e.g., conveying only commander's intent, as in the case of self-synchronization).

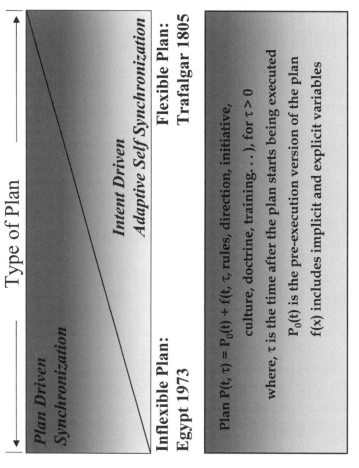

Figure 69. What Is the Role of Planning in Synchronization?

Commander's Intent

The quality of commanders and their ideas are crucial to the whole theory of command and control. Builder, Bankes, and Nordin make a strong argument for this concept[4] which is familiar to those who study U.S. doctrine.

The qualities of commanders and their ideas are more important to a general theory of command and control than the technical and architectural qualities of their sensors, computers, and communications systems. This theory separates the art of command and control from the hardware and software systems that support command and control. It centers on the idea of a command concept, a commander's vision of a military operation that informs the making of command decisions during that operation. The theory suggests that the essential communications up and down the chain of command can (and should) be limited to disseminating, verifying, or modifying these crucial command concepts. The theory also suggests, as an extreme case, that an ideal command concept is one that is so prescient, sound, and fully conveyed to subordinates that it would allow the commander to leave the battlefield before the battle commences, with no adverse effect upon the outcome. This theory, developed by Builder, et al., through six historical case studies of modern battles, explores the implications of both the professional development of commanders and the design and evaluation of command and control architectures. The theory should be of interest to those involved in developing command and control doctrine for the U.S. military and to those interested in the military art and science of command and control.

What Type of C2 Concept Is Appropriate for a Given Mission?

It is important to note that no single C2 concept is right for all situations. The ideal choice of C2 concept, within the spectrum described earlier, will depend upon a number of factors including the complexity of the operation, the capability of the forces, the command culture, and the quality of the supporting information systems. Establishing rules to guide the selection of an effective C2 concept is a current topic of exploration within the research community. However, as indicated in Figure 70, some general trends and bounds have been conjectured by Perrow and others as a result of a study of control strategies to minimize accidents associated with complex systems.[5]

C2 Approaches

Fully Centralized	Centralized Command / Decentralized Control	Collaborative C2	Decentralized C2 (Self Synchronization)	No Organization

Perrow Quadrants (Interactions/Coupling and Centralization/Decentralization)

Centralized	Either	Decentralized	Neither
Linear/Tight	Linear/Loose	Complex/Loose	Complex/Tight

Nonlinearity Spectrum

Equilibrium	Mildly Complex	Complex	Chaos

Historical Military Emphasis   **Emerging e-commerce Emphasis**

Figure 70. What Type of C2 Concept Is Appropriate for a Given Mission?

Perrow characterized the variation in system complexity by two factors: type of interaction and degree of coupling. The type of interaction was defined as linear or complex; in the linear case, the relationship among the key variables is transparent and the events predictable; in the case of complex systems, small changes in key variables can cause big changes in outcome and unexpected events can occur in spite of system design.

The degree of coupling was described as either loose or tight, where loose meant ambiguous interfaces with significant slack that provided flexibility, and tight implied a high level of interdependence with closely specified tolerances that resulted in rigid interfaces.

Perrow concluded from his analysis that centralized control approaches were appropriate for systems with linear interactions and tight coupling, and decentralized control was better suited for systems with complex interactions and loose coupling. *While either approach could be used for systems that were characterized by linear interaction and loose coupling, it is important to note that for systems with complex interaction and tight coupling, neither is appropriate.*

This correlates with the findings from the theory of complex adaptive systems that decentralized approaches are better suited for more complex systems. However, at the high-end of the nonlinearity spectrum, systems are in a state of chaos and cannot be controlled with any strategy. These conjectures suggest that, depending upon the situation, there could exist fundamental limits to our ability to synchronize forces in military operations. The challenge is to characterize these situations in a meaningful way that will aid in understanding the level of complexity involved and the appropriate type of C2 concept.

While analyses of synchronization and its role in Information Age Warfare remains in a very early state, several conjectures (not yet rising to the level of testable hypotheses) have emerged from the work to date and appear worthy of investigation. They include:

- The degree of synchronization of a system can be characterized by the level of aggregation at which the behavior of its entities can be predicted or controlled.

- The maximum degree of synchronization achievable is limited by the inherent complexity of the system whose entities are being synchronized.

- The actual level of synchronization achieved is influenced by:

    - Degree of centralization/decentralization of C2 concept; and

    - Extent to which entities are networked.

- Increased networking enables decentralized C2 concepts that maximize synchronization for a given level of system complexity.

Some Hypotheses

The discussion up to this point suggests a number of hypotheses that need to be explored systematically and rigorously by the DoD. Examples of statements that seem worthy of experimental focus are identified and discussed below:

- Higher degrees of synchronization will result in improved operational effectiveness and/or efficiency.

- Increases in networking enable decentralized C2 concepts that maximize the degree of synchronization achievable for a given level of system complexity.

- Increases in the quality and sharing of information and the degree of collaboration will result in improved synchronization when decentralized C2 concepts are employed.

These statements reflect the potential relationships and benefits implied by the earlier qualitative discussion and, as such, represent a useful starting point for exploration.

However, it is important to point out that Information Superiority capabilities such as quality of information, degree of information sharing, and collaboration are enablers and do not generate operational benefits by themselves. It is also important to understand (1) the factors that can keep potential operational benefits from being achieved, and (2) the operational conditions under which the enabling Information Superiority capabilities themselves are likely to be attained. In either case, it is necessary to define the key attributes and metrics necessary to design and conduct experiments to explore and test these hypotheses so that we will be better able to understand the key relationships, factors, and conditions that characterize them.

Illustrative Attributes for Key Information Superiority Concepts Related to Hypotheses Regarding Synchronization

Figure 71 depicts the relationship among Information Superiority concepts as embodied in the collection of hypotheses related to synchronization. It also includes examples of attributes that need to be measured in order to explore these hypotheses. Networking and coordination are enablers and their attributes (and metrics) have already been discussed. The command and control concept is also an enabler. While the attributes of centralization and decentralization have been discussed, the metrics associated with these organizational characteristics deserve attention. One example of a metric for measuring the degree of centralization or decentralization of a command and control concept is the number of actions taken on the basis of situation information versus those taken on orders from higher authority. The attributes of synchronization itself (i.e., the degree of synchronization and agility and the associated metrics) will be the focus of the remainder of this section. The degree of operational success and force effectiveness or efficiency are attributes of the operation that must be measured in order to determine the value of various levels of synchronization.

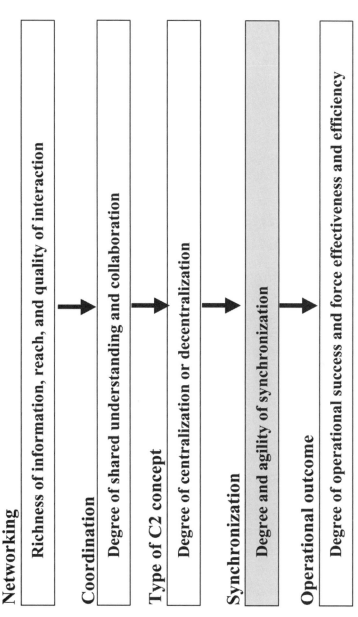

Networking

Richness of information, reach, and quality of interaction

Coordination

Degree of shared understanding and collaboration

Type of C2 concept

Degree of centralization or decentralization

Synchronization

Degree and agility of synchronization

Operational outcome

Degree of operational success and force effectiveness and efficiency

Figure 71. Illustrative Attributes for Key Information Superiority Concepts Related to Hypotheses Regarding Synchronization

Note that the five levels depicted in Figure 71 reflect the hierarchy of measures of merit. Networking itself, made up of richness, reach, and quality of interaction, should be addressed by measures of performance (MOP). Coordination and the appropriateness of the C2 concept are issues at the level of C4ISR measures of effectiveness (MOE). Synchronization and the operational outcome, however, are reality domain issues and should be assessed using measures of force effectiveness (MOFE) and/or measures of policy effectiveness (MOPE).

Measuring the Degree of Synchronization

In constructing a measure of the degree of synchronization achieved by an organization in the conduct of a particular operation, one must ensure that the measure accurately reflects the concept not only at a given point in time, but also the ability to maintain synchronization throughout the operation.

First, let us consider a static measure of synchronization based upon the concepts introduced so far. To begin with, there are a finite number of independent entities involved in an operation at a given point in time. Each of these entities is related to every other entity in one of three ways. That is, any two entities can be in a state of interference, neutrality, or synergy. For example, take the situation where there are three entities: A, B, and C. We can easily anchor three points on a scale (1, 0, -1). Perfect synchronization, with a value of +1, would mean that all three of these entities are cooperating; that is, all of the pair-wise relationships (in this case there are two AB and AC) are in a state of synergy. A perfect lack of synchronization, with a value of −1, would involve all of these pair-wise relationships in a state of interference. The origin, with a value of 0, represents a case when all pair-wise relationships are in a state of neutrality. The following formula generates the above values for the situations described above.

$$S = \frac{\sum_{\iota = 1}^{n-1} V\iota}{C^n_2}$$

where,

S = degree of synchronization [-1≤S≤+1]
C^n_2 = combination of n things taken 2 at a time
Vι =   1 if the ιth pair is in a state of synergy
           0 if the ιth pair is in a state of neutrality
           -1 if the ιth pair is in a state of interference
n = case number

Our simple example can take on only seven different values for S even though there are 21 individual situations (cases) that can occur. Figure 72 depicts the 27 unique situations (3^n) that could occur and how these situations map to the seven possible values. Clearly, the number of possible situations that could occur increases dramatically as n increases.

Cases

Pair	1	2	3	4	5	6	7	8	9	10	11	12	13	14	15	16	17	18	19	20	21	22	23	24	25	26	27
AB	-1	-1	-1	0	-1	0	0	-1	-1	1	0	-1	0	0	-1	+1	+1	1	0	0	1	1	-1	1	1	0	1
AC	-1	-1	0	-1	0	-1	0	-1	1	-1	0	0	-1	+1	+1	0	-1	0	1	0	0	-1	1	1	0	1	1
BC	-1	0	-1	-1	0	0	-1	1	-1	-1	0	+1	+1	-1	0	-1	0	0	0	1	-1	1	0	0	1	1	1
ΣVt	-3	-2	-2	-2	-1	-1	-1	-1	-1	-1	0	0	0	0	0	0	0	1	1	1	1	1	1	2	2	2	3
S	-1	◄— -2/3 —►			◄— -1/3 —►						◄— 0 —►							◄— 1/3 —►						◄— 2/3 —►			1

$$S = C_2^3 = \frac{3!}{2!\,1!} = \frac{3*2*1}{2*1*1} = 3$$

Figure 72. Synchronization Value

It should be noted that imbedded in these 21 situations (that were generated by considering pair wise states) are two instances of three-way interactions (cases 1 and 27). As n gets larger there will be a number of cases that include synergies and/or interferences involving more than two entities. This formula weights these multiple synergies and/or interferences linearity; that is, a three-way synergy is 50 percent better than a two-way synergy. In reality this may or may not be the case. We anticipate that the results of analyses and experiments will tell us whether or not this measure, S, needs to be refined to reflect an exponential weighing for n-way interactions. We would suggest we use this measure for the time being because the relative simplicity of this measure will encourage its use in practice, which represents significant progress in the state of practice in being able to quantitatively describe synchronization and its impacts on mission effectiveness.

Having developed a static measure of synchronization, we need to consider how to measure the ability of an organization to maintain synchronization over the course of an operation. Figure 73 tracks the level of synchronization achieved over time for each of three operations. These illustrative curves show why a measure of the average level of synchronization would, by itself, not be a particularly useful measure. To understand how well synchronization was maintained over the course of an operation, a measure of the variation in levels achieved over time is needed. To understand whether or not we were able to improve synchronization over time, the average slope of the curve would be useful. Those following three measures, taken together, provide a preliminary understanding of the degree of synchronization achieved in an operation.

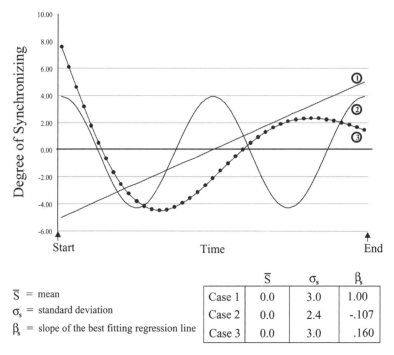

Figure 73. Synchronization Profiles

	$\overline{S}$	σ_s	β_s
Case 1	0.0	3.0	1.00
Case 2	0.0	2.4	-.107
Case 3	0.0	3.0	.160

$\overline{S}$ = mean

σ_s = standard deviation

β_s = slope of the best fitting regression line

Figure 74 illustrates the value of these measures for the curves (cases) depicted in Figure 73. Having these synchronization measures available will enable us to characterize the nature of synchronization achieved with a given concept of operations, C2 approach, C2 system, etc., and thereby contribute to a better understanding of how these mission capability package design elements relate to mission effectiveness.

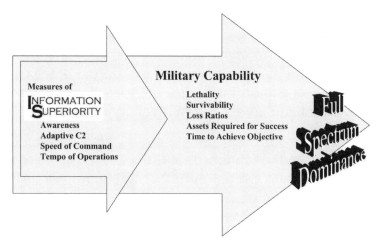

Figure 74. Growing Body of Evidence

Temporal Aspects of Synchronization

Both the time to make and communicate decisions necessary for synchronization (e.g., collecting information, planning or scheduling of activities, or collaborative decisionmaking among force elements), as well as the time required for forces themselves to be properly arranged, must be considered. Contrary to frequent objections this is not a cost, but an attribute of a method of synchronization and should be treated separately.

Cost of Synchronization

While a high degree of synchronization can, depending upon the mission, have significant benefits in terms of increased effectiveness or efficiency, any different level of synchronization also has costs that must be understood and measured.

One cost that can be incurred with increased levels of synchronization is reduced robustness. High degrees of synchronization generally require dependence on information and the associated infrastructure that provides it. Both of these could be potentially disrupted or degraded by an adversary. Also, as the precision of synchronization increases so does sensitivity to errors that can creep in from a variety of sources.

The degree to which the costs that are associated with achieving synchronization are considered significant (and worthy of further attention) will vary with the degree of synchronization required, type of C2 employed, and the particular operation undertaken. These ideas need further development.

Concepts for Experiments

The metrics described here could be used in a series of experiments to test the validity of the hypotheses postulated earlier. This could be achieved by means of the following three step approach:

1. Develop an initial set of alternative C2 concepts that vary in the degree of centralization/ decentralization. These options could be similar to those discussed earlier.

2. Evaluate the impact of these options on a spectrum of operations that vary in complexity by including such factors as number of force elements, degree of coupling, and the dynamics of operation.

3. For each alternative, vary key parameters relative to Information Superiority. These should include: quality of commander's intent, quality of

situation information, degree of information sharing, and degree of collaboration.

Because of the broad ranging scope of the hypotheses, this experimentation process should be viewed as a long-term, multiphase undertaking that allows for the evolution of C2 concepts as experience is gained. Analytic discovery experiments could be used to help focus limited objective laboratory tests, as well as broad field experiments. Over time, the exploration process could migrate across the spectrum of missions/operations. Consistency in the broad types of C2 concepts assessed and the metrics used for evaluation would permit the development of a body of knowledge that would contribute to an understanding of the conditions under which the hypotheses might be true and provide a basis for establishing a set of best practices for tailoring C2 processes to the situation at hand.

---

[1]*Merriam-Webster's Collegiate Dictionary*, Tenth Edition (Springfield, MA: Merriam-Webster, Inc., 1995).

[2]Robert G. Tanner, *Stonewall in the Valley: Thomas J. "Stonewall" Jackson's Shenandoah Valley Campaign, Spring 1862* (Mechanicsville, PA: Stackpole Books, 1996).

[3]"Systematic Assessment of C2 Effectiveness and Its Determinants," *Proceedings of the 1994 Symposium on Command and Control Research and Decision Aids* (June 1994), pp. 425-452.

[4]C.H. Builder, S.C. Bankes, and R. Nordin, *Command Concepts: A Theory Derived from the Practice of Command and Control* (RAND Corp. MR-775-OSD, 1999).

[5]Charles Perrow, *Normal Accidents: Living with High Risk Technologies* (New York: Basic Books, Inc., 1984). Thomas J. Czerwinski, *Coping with the Bounds: Speculations on Nonlinearity in Military Affairs* (Washington, DC: National Defense University Press, 1998).

CHAPTER 10

Growing Body of Evidence

There is a growing body of evidence that provides an existence proof for the validity of each of the different classes of Network Centric Warfare hypotheses (delineated in Chapter 4).

- Hypotheses of the first class deal with the relationships among information sharing, improved awareness, and shared awareness.

- Hypotheses in the second class include those that involve the relationship between shared awareness and synchronization. For example, the effect of different degrees of shared awareness or collaboration on synchronization.

- The third class of hypotheses involves the link between synchronization and mission effectiveness.

The most compelling evidence identified to date exists at the tactical level in a broad range of mission areas. This evidence has been assembled from a variety of Service and combined experimentation and operational demonstrations, as well as high-intensity, tactical conflict situations. The following examples identified are supported by the relationships between:

- Improved networking capabilities and increased information sharing

- Increased information sharing and increased shared situational awareness

- Increased shared situational awareness and improved collaboration and synchronization

- Increased mission effectiveness as a result of the presence of one or more of these factors

The strongest evidence uncovered to date exists in seven mission areas: air-to-air, maneuver, Counter Special Operations Forces (CSOF), theater air and missile defense (TAMD), strike, and split-based operations. Figure 75 provides a framework for organizing the evidence.

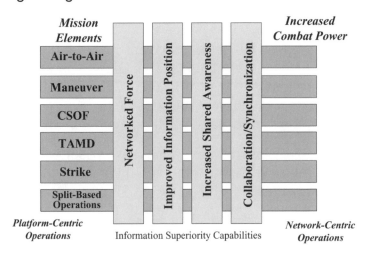

Figure 75. Assessment of the Emerging Evidence

Evaluating the Evidence and Measuring Maturity of Network Centric Warfare Concepts

The maturity of a network-centric application is related to the interaction between two key dimensions: the degree to which the command and control system (including the humans as part of that system) is able to share information and develop shared situational awareness and the degree to which that same system (including the doctrine and organizational elements of the system) is able to move toward self-synchronized forces. The patterns resulting from the interaction of these two dimensions are illustrated in Figure 76 which labels the expected progression of Network Centric Warfare capabilities with values from 0 through 4.

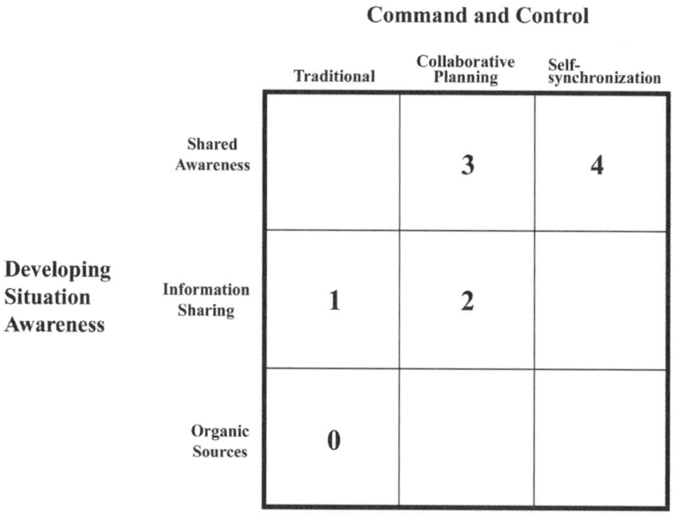

Command and Control

	Traditional	Collaborative Planning	Self-synchronization
Shared Awareness		3	4
Developing Situation Awareness — Information Sharing	1	2	
Organic Sources	0		

Figure 76. Network Centric Maturity Model

Each of the values for the maturity of a network-centric warfighting capability is defined by considering these two aspects of network-centric behavior. The first, the process of developing shared situational awareness, is meant to be a reflection of the degree to which information and awareness are shared. The second, the nature of command and control, is meant as a surrogate for how shared awareness is leveraged. Platform-centric operations anchor the network-centric warfare value at 0. At the other end of this scale (value 4) are mature network-centric operations that involve widespread information sharing, the development of a fully integrated common operational picture (COP) that promotes shared awareness, collaborative planning processes, and a self-synchronizing approach to command and control.

Moving from Value 0 (platform-centric operations) to Network Centric Warfare maturity Value 1 involves the ability to share information. Information sharing is assumed to be associated with improved awareness. Moving from Value 1 to Value 2 involves the addition of some form of collaborative planning among the participants. Movement from Value 2 to Value 3 involves richer collaboration, involving more actors and integrating more aspects of the operation. In many cases, there is less communication among the participants because of the shared situational awareness achieved (though early in the process of learning to collaborate, there may be more. In addition, cases have been reported where communication stays the same, but has richer content). Movement from Value 3 to Value 4 requires a mission capability package that allows integration across doctrine, organization, training, material, and other aspects of the force and its supporting systems that permit self-synchronization.

The ability to conduct network-centric operations can vary widely depending on the capabilities of the forces, the command and control systems that support them, and the command arrangements. A useful analogy for describing these concepts is provided by soccer. Soccer has few rules and few opportunities to restart the play on favorable terms. Each player must be aware of the field, who has control of the ball and where it is on the field, the capabilities and positions of the other players (friendly and adversary), and the dynamic interactions among those factors. Young players are taught to play specific roles and to react to standard situations. More experienced players are given both more freedom and more responsibilities—for example, defenders are taught to recognize opportunities to slip forward into the attack and create numerical and positional advantages for their team. At the highest level of soccer the play is fluid, with constantly changing shapes for both the attack and the defense. Their ability to read and react to these dynamics, with minimal verbal communication (for example, calling for the ball attracts the attention of the defense), often determines match outcomes.

Of course, Network Centric Warfare concepts are much more complex than soccer, which has only 11 players on a side. Network Centric Warfare situations can vary greatly in size and complexity, from single service squads at the tactical level to theater-level joint forces and coalition operations. The examples of Network Centric Warfare concepts and capabilities described in this chapter vary in scope and complexity from tactical air-to-air engagements (1 vs. 1 to 8 vs. 16) to multi-brigade ground maneuvers with 7,000 plus soldiers opposed by an active OPFOR. In addition, the degree to which the various elements of the force have been networked varies considerably, as well as degree to which information sharing and shared situational awareness were achieved. In addition, the maturity of the tactics, techniques, and procedures employed by the forces varied from very changes in TT&P to new TT&P that effectively leverage the power of the network.

The maturity matrix combined with the scope and scale of network-centric applications will allow us to interpret these examples and measure progress toward a force with network-centric warfighting capabilities.

Air-to-Air Mission: Offensive and Defensive Counter

Compelling evidence exists in the air-to-air mission area for the Network Centric Warfare linkage hypotheses. In this mission area, the networking of sensors and shooters with data links, such as Link-16, enables a force to operate in the network-centric region of the information domain. The improved information position that can be achieved with networking is portrayed in Figure 77.

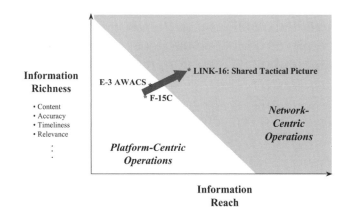

Figure 77. Air-to-Air: Improved Information Position

The tactical foundation for the air-to-air mission consists of Basic Flight Maneuver (BFM) Tactics. These tactics call for a pilot to first observe an adversary with onboard sensors or the naked eye. Then the pilot predicts a course of maneuver for the enemy based on an assessment of the adversary's energy state, knowledge of the enemy's tactics, aircraft, and relative advantage in position. Next, the pilot assesses a maneuver needed for himself in order to defeat an adversary's or counter an adversary's defensive move while on the offensive. Finally, a maneuver is accomplished with great speed, which is designed to be unpredictable. This cycle is repeated as required through the engagement. If a pilot is capable of maneuvering with enough quickness that an adversary cannot react with appropriate counter-maneuver, then he or she will be decisive.[1] The tactics described above are referred to as OPAM, for Observe, Predict, Assess, and Maneuver (a rephrasing of the Observe, Orient, Decide, and Act loop, from which they are derived). In the rest of this volume, the classic OODA formulation is used.

Salient aspects of the tactics described above can be represented graphically, as shown in Figure 78, using the primitives discussed previously in Chapter 2. This representation of two coupled OODA loops can represent either two pilots or pilot and controller sharing information via voice traffic. Air controllers are typically located on command and control aircraft such as an E-3 AWACS (Airborne Warning and Control System), or in typical naval operations an E-2 Hawkeye that carries a broad area sensor. Their systems typically form the basis for the information position available to controllers for observing and orienting.

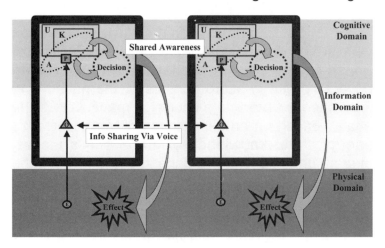

Figure 78. Coupled OODA Loops: Voice Only

Consider the tactical situation in the 4 vs. 4 engagement portrayed in Figure 79. A representative platform-centric information position that is available to a fighter pilot via heads-up display is portrayed on the left side of Figure 80. In this operational situation, the lead aircraft in Blue's defensive formation can only see those Red aircraft in a very narrow field of view directly to its front—the zone covered by its onboard radar. Consequently, when orienting and trying to establish the general positions, speeds, and vectors of attacking and defending aircraft, the pilot must combine his organic information position with information communicated by voice from other pilots or controllers. His orientation is facilitated by knowledge of Blue and potentially Red tactics, techniques, or procedures (TTPs) as well as preflight mission briefs.

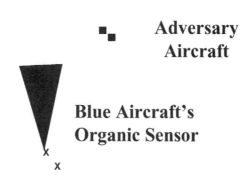

Adversary Aircraft

Blue Aircraft's Organic Sensor

Blue Aircraft

Figure 79. Air-to-Air: Tactical Situation: 4 vs. 4

Prior to tactical closure, controllers are cycling through the OODA process and sharing information with pilots via voice as they vector fighter aircraft to an attack positions and attempt to put Blue pilots in the most advantageous attack positions while simultaneously attempting to control the actions of all the defending aircraft to ensure that a sound defensive posture is maintained. If these command and control platforms are not available, direction may come from a surface vessel or ground control radar station. If this control function is not performed, mission performance may be degraded for one or more of the following reasons:

• Attacking aircraft may slip through the defensive screen because the organic sensors of the defending aircraft themselves are short range and local, leaving gaps in coverage. This can result in leakers or attack aircraft that penetrate the air defenses.

• To compensate for the lack of control, more aircraft may have to be put on station to detect and intercept attacking aircraft, resulting in lower operational tempo and less efficient use of assets.

• Speed of tactical decisionmaking may be slower with respect to the pace of the air-to-air battle because information about attacking aircraft will take longer to generate and deliver to those who need it.

• Loss ratios may be less favorable because interceptions occur under less favorable conditions.

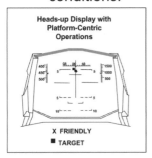

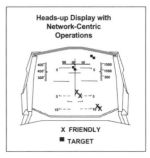

Warfighter View which results from sharing info via <u>voice only</u> communications

Warfighter View which results from sharing info via <u>voice and data</u> communications

Figure 80. Voice vs. Voice Plus Data Links

In contrast to platform-centric operations, which are dominated by voice traffic, network-centric operations are dominated by data traffic augmented by voice. The networking of sensors and shooters with data links such as Link-16 creates a robustly networked force that has the ability to share information among all platforms and create significantly improved information positions vis-à-vis platform-centric operations.

The source of the increase in combat power that can result from the ability to share digital information can be understood by once again employing the primitives. Figure 81 portrays two coupled OODAs that can correspond to two pilots, or a pilot and a controller. It is clear from this diagram that the OODA loops of these two individuals are tightly coupled because the data link allows the pilots to share crucial data and information on a continuing basis. If the sensors of one aircraft detect a target (observe), then this track information can be shared along with position information of both Blue aircraft. The result of information sharing is a dramatically improved information position, which is portrayed in Figure 82.

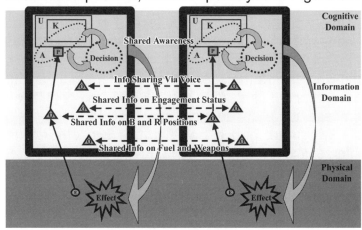

Figure 81. Coupled OODA Loops: Voice Plus Data

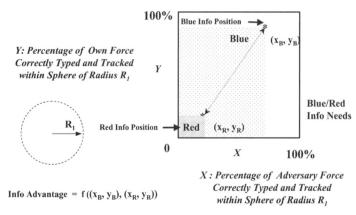

Figure 82. Air-to-Air: Relative Information Advantage

This dramatically improved information position allows Blue force pilots and controllers to orient on the same position location information. The sharing of additional information, such as weapons loading and fuel status, as well as the status of the current engagement, results in the creation of a significant information advantage. This information advantage enables pilots and controllers to more rapidly orient themselves by using common information. This has several observable effects. Most obviously, the information directly available to every pilot to orient with is richer. For example, the heads-up display on the right side of Figure 80 illustrates the fact that the lead Blue pilot now has a richer view of the Red aircraft (he sees all four of them, not just the two in front of him). As a result, during the orientation process, the pilot can more effectively locate himself, his wingman, and a trail flight of two other blue interceptors to form a mental three-dimensional picture. This picture can be merged with other engagement information, prior knowledge (e.g., the capabilities of each type of aircraft involved in the action), and situation understanding (from mission briefings, etc.) to create improved situational awareness.

This improved situational awareness enables two or more pilots (and others on the network) to form similar mental patterns of the engagement that aid them in tactical decisionmaking (decide) and influences Blue pilot actions (act) in several important ways. First, the pilots themselves can make decisions that are mutually reinforcing about how to approach the Red aircraft and gain advantageous positions for the interception and battle that follows. Second, they can see one another's actions. As a result, the trail flight can act independently and intelligently to support the actions of the lead flight. Perhaps equally important, there is less talk on the radio. Rather than having to vector aircraft and describe what cannot be seen via voice, the supporting platforms are largely just feeding basic information over Link-16. This reduces the load on the controllers, and very importantly, reduces the cognitive load on the pilots of the interceptors. Less voice traffic is needed, which means pilots can concentrate on the battlespace and their actions.

The overall effect is one that enables the pilots to self-synchronize their efforts, though they also have the ability to talk with one another and the controllers. At a minimum, these pilots have the capacity to increase their awareness of the battlespace and, in theory, to greatly improve their shared awareness since they all see the additional information.

The operational benefit of employing F15-C aircraft equipped with Link-16 was explored in an Operational Special Project (OSP) undertaken by the U.S. Air Force during the 1990s. The JTIDS OSP compared mission effectiveness for voice only vs. voice plus Link-16 in a wide range of tactical situations (1 vs. 1 to 8 vs. 16) in day and night operations. Data was collected during more than 12,000 sorties and 19,000 flying hours. In daylight operations, the average kill ratio increased from 3.10:1 to 8.11:1, a 2.61 x improvement. During night operations the average kill ratio increased from 3.62:1 to 9.40:1, a 2.59 improvement.[2] For both day and night operations, this translates to an increase of over 150 percent, a major gain by any standard. While the actual increases in awareness and shared awareness were not measured, the observables reported anecdotally (less use of tactical radios, supporting maneuvers without discussion, etc.) support the conclusion that there were significant changes in these attributes of the cognitive domain.

At the qualitative level, the JTIDS OSP Report to Congress summarized the impact of data links to augment voice communications in air-to-air combat in this way:

- Each flight member was able to see the disposition of flight members, regardless of their separation.

- This shared awareness made split tactics easier, led to greater flight effectiveness, and afforded quicker rejoins when desired.

- The mutual support enhancements proved even more significant against a non-equipped adversary in night and weather conditions since the adversary formation either had to stay together or substantially degrade mutual support.

- When voice was used, the pilots often referred to a common picture making the voice more meaningful.

- In testing with the data link, a perfect sort was routine with four (and two) ship flights. This had strong positive implications concerning first pass kill results, fighting outnumbered, survivability, and cost effectiveness employing expensive aircraft/missiles. When an F-15 inadvertently locked onto another flight member, the error was graphically displayed (by the lock line going to the friendly fighter), and the pilot lost little time in determining the error and avoiding possible fratricide.[3]

The relevant values for information sharing, improved information position, shared awareness, increased OPTEMPO, and an increased kill ratio (for daylight operations) are portrayed in Figure 83. Embedded in this relationship are the new tactics, techniques, and procedures that were developed by the pilots that participated in the JTIDS OSP to dramatically increase combat power by taking advantage of improved shared awareness.

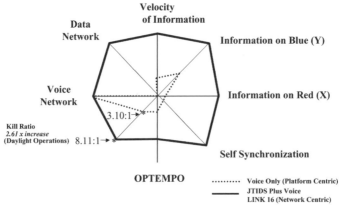

Figure 83. Air-to-Air

Maneuver

The evidence from exercise, experiments, and analyses that have dealt explicitly with maneuver demonstrates both the challenges and payoffs of network-centric operations. During the early phases of experimentation, U.S. Army units were not able to field a high performance tactical network or develop and employ mature TTPs that could enable them to leverage high quality shared awareness. However, the recently completed Division Capstone Exercise— Phase I showcased the increased combat power that maneuver forces employing more mature Network Centric Warfare capabilities can achieve. The discussion that follows clearly highlights the progress the Army has made in understanding both the challenges and the opportunities faced by maneuver forces in leveraging the power of the network.

The U.S. Army's Advanced Warfighting Experiments (AWEs) have been key to putting digital technologies on the battlefield. These experiments, as well as experiments conducted by U.S. Army battle laboratories and research and development centers, have provided the Army with a means for exploring and gaining insight into the feasibility of Network Centric Warfare technologies and the related doctrinal and organizational implications. AWEs have provided valuable lessons learned as well as some of the first analytical underpinnings to support the theory of Network Centric Warfare as a combat multiplier.

The U.S. Army conducts a variety of activities under the umbrella of Advanced Warfighting Experiments (AWEs). They conduct staged engagements at the Brigade level with experimental systems, capabilities, and concepts (e.g., Task Force XXI). They also conduct Command Post Exercises (CPXs) with real staffs and real command and control systems and simulated forces (e.g. Division AWE). In addition, they also conduct extensive analyses and simulations (e.g., pre- and post-experimentation analysis as they did before and after the Task Force XXI AWE). The results of these different kinds of experiments and exercises are not strictly comparable, but a careful examination of their findings provides support for the hypotheses discussed earlier.

The U.S. Army's first Advanced Warfighting Experiment(AWEs), the Desert Hammer VI AWE, was conducted in April of 1994. The purpose of this initial AWE was to examine the impacts of a Battalion Task Force with digital communications across each Battlefield Operating System (BOS). The results of this AWE, and several subsequent AWEs, when viewed in hindsight, highlight the significant progress the U.S. Army has made in developing and maturing Network Centric Warfare capabilities. The anticipated benefits of digitization and networking: increased lethality, survivability, and OPTEMPO were slow to materialize in initial experiments. A number of factors were identified that influenced the divergence between potential performance and observed performance. These factors formed the basis for insights and lessons learned that paved the way for future success. These insights included:

- The importance of a high performance communications network

- The need for adequate training with new digital capabilities

- The importance of unit collective training time with digital capabilities

- The importance of limiting the number of capabilities introduced prior to a given experiment

- The need to screen digital capabilities for maturity.[4]

The Task Force XXI Advanced Warfighting Experiment (AWE) was conducted at the National Training Center (NTC), Fort Irwin, California in March of 1997. Although the results from the Task Force XXI AWE were less than conclusive, the results of the Division AWE conducted at Fort Hood in 1997, subsequent training operations with digitized forces after the Task Force XXI AWE, the results of Allied exercises, and Phase I of the Division Capstone Exercise conducted in April of 2001 have highlighted that significant gains in combat power that can be achieved with network-centric operations.

Task Force XXI AWE

The objective of Task Force XXI was to explore whether a digitized force with properly integrated doctrine and technologies would attain increases in lethality, operational tempo and survivability. Task Force XXI was the first effort to integrate tactical radios with commercially based routers, thus providing a networking capability at lower echelons to rapidly share common situation awareness. The Army demonstrated technologies that shared friendly situational awareness down to the individual platform level, improved command and control, and, for the first time, showed that time-sensitive information could be shared horizontally rather than having to follow the traditional chain of command path.

Task Force XXI also demonstrated the power of networking multiple sensors and rapidly turning sensor data into useful information. The full range of digital weather support was delivered from garrison to the field through satellite communications links. The division Analytical Control Element received battlefield information from maneuver unit spot reports and various Army and Joint sensor platforms. Analysts used the All-Source Analysis System to correlate and fuse this information into a coherent, timely enemy picture that was used to update the COP not only at the TOC but also down to the individual digitized weapons platform. For the first time, soldiers in the tank could see what was happening around them. The Experimental Force (EXFOR) for the Task Force XXI AXE consisted of an armor battalion, a mechanized infantry battalion, a light infantry battalion, and various support units. Within the EXFOR's two heavy maneuver battalions were 873 digitized and networked platforms, consisting of M1A1 tanks and M2A2 Bradley fighting vehicles equipped with appliques. The EXFOR's light infantry battalion contained 186 dismounted soldier systems and was equipped with the Javelin anti-tank missile system. A battalion M109A6 Paladins provided field artillery support, and the Aviation Task Force consisted of eight AH-4A Apaches, two AH-64D Apache Longbows, and eight OH-58 Kiowa Warriors.

The EXFOR prepared for the AWE at Fort Hood by conducting platoon, company, and battalion collective training, as well as a culminating brigade exercise that took place in December of 1996. During this training, a significant amount of time was dedicated to the mastery of the hardware and software that digitized and networked the platforms. An undesirable consequence of this focus on new hardware and software was a decrease in the time available for unit training.

During the AWE, the EXFOR conducted a total of eight missions against the opposing OPFOR at the NTC. These missions included: movement to contact, deliberate attack, and hasty defense. Of the eight missions, three were similar to missions conducted by non-digitized forces during normal training rotations, and five were characterized as unique missions designed for the digital force. The size of EXFOR was relatively constant for all eight missions and tactics employed by the EXFOR did not vary significantly across the missions. However, the EXFOR was dispersed to a greater degree than normal during the five unique missions.

The performance of the EXFOR's network during the AWE was limited by hardware and software problems, which resulted in an information position that was significantly degraded from what could have been achieved with a higher performance network. For example, the message completion rate for digital message traffic was under 30 percent. The net result was that situational awareness did not increase to the degree achieved in the air-to-air mission in the JTIDS OSP. However, it is interesting to note that the most significant Blue victory, which took place in the final battle, was directly attributable to the excellent performance of UAVs linked to the attack helicopters during the battle. This gave the Blue force a local information advantage that they were able to effectively exploit. These results were similar to outcomes observed in most rotations at the NTC. However, one of the key observations made by the EXFOR was the value of increased Blue situational awareness that was resulted from the use of the tactical Internet, with about 75 percent of platoons visible at the battalion command post. This increased positional location capability was used by combat support units to find the vehicles they needed to rearm and refuel, as well as mark and avoid minefields and chemical strike areas. In addition, shared positional information helped artillery units see with some certainty the location of the friendly forces, which assisted them in clearing fires.

U.S. Army Division AWE

The U.S. Army conducted a Division AWE at Fort Hood in 1997 with the objective of determining the warfighting effectiveness of a digitized division-sized force. This AWE was conducted over a period of 9 days with elements of an Infantry Division in the context of a Battle Command Training Program (BCTP) command post exercise. This exercise differed from previous exercises in that it was conducted largely through the use of the Corps Battle Simulation, a computer-assisted wargame. The focus of the exercise was the command and control of digitized forces. Consequently, all units smaller than command posts were simulated, and the division and brigade command posts were deployed in the garrison area of Fort Hood and connected via radio and landline links.

The Division AWE wide area network architecture employed at Fort Hood was up to 48 times faster than the wide area network developed for Task Force XXI. Similarly, local area networks inside each Division AWE command post were markedly better than those used in Task Force XXI. This augmented network supported additional applications such as video teleconferencing and higher volume, faster data transfers. The network also supported previously used network applications, such as exchanging formatted messages, client-server operations, and web-based operations.

As in Task Force XXI, there were striking examples during the Division AWE of commanders and staff members perceiving the battlespace with greater clarity than ever before and then acting on that perception with great speed. This time, digitization of the battlefield led to the Experimental Force (EXFOR) achieving and sustaining situational awareness and information dominance over the World Class Opposing Force (WCOF). In turn, this permitted the Experimental Force to conduct distributed, non-contiguous operations over an extended battlefield. As the enemy attempted to maneuver, the Experimental Force was able to locate and track the enemy's most critical forces and bring massed, destructive fires on them. The subsequent close fight allowed cohesive, mobile Experimental Force brigade combat teams (BCTs) to engage and defeat the disrupted and attrited Opposing Force units.

Despite numerous problems along the lines of those discussed previously (software interoperability problems, need for adequate training on new command and control systems) the following improvements relative to the results of previous warfighters (CPXs) were observed:

- Operational tempo: division-level plan development time was reduced from 72 hours to 12 hours, making a six-fold increase in OPTEMPO possible.

- Speed of calls for fire: time required for processing calls for fire was reduced from 3 minutes to 0.5 minutes, again a six-fold increase in the potential for bringing fire assets to bear, with increased potential lethality as well as potential for saving friendly lives and improving the pace of battle or friendly OPTEMPO.

- Planning time for deliberate attacks at the company level was cut in half, from 40 to 20 minutes. Substantial improvements in OPTEMPO and the ability to operate within the adversary's OODA loop were therefore demonstrated.[5]

UK Exercise Big Picture 1

In February of 1997 UK Exercise Big Picture 1 (BP1) demonstrated the potential combat power that can be generated with a networked ground force. BP1 was conducted at Grafenwoehr Simulation Center with a UK squadron/company level unit in a simulated environment that overcame many of the observed limitations of the tactical Internet. During the exercise, 18 tank simulators and 17 infantry fighting vehicle simulators were hardwired in an attempt to replicate a level of network performance that could theoretically be achieved with a high performance tactical Internet. Each simulated digitized platform contained full color map displays and a touch screen. In addition, a robust experimental design methodology was employed to remove the effects of geography, level of training, and unit in the estimation of performance gains from digitization. These simulators were then manned, and various tactical missions were conducted. A key observation made by the UK soldiers who participated in the experiment was the tremendous value of increased situational awareness of blue forces that was realized through digitization and networking. The following results were observed in comparison to similar simulations with non-digitized forces:[6]

- Survivability/Lethality: Blue force suffered up to 50 percent fewer losses as a proportion of the total kills inflicted in the attack mission

- OPTEMPO: Mean time to complete the command and control phase of the attacks was 40 percent lower

Observations From U.S. Army Training Exercises

Numerous training exercises conducted with digitized U.S. Army units have shed insight into the validity of individual components of the Network Centric Warfare hypotheses. As research and experimentation proceed, it is expected that these qualitative insights will be converted into quantifiable findings.

Value of Increased Shared Situational Awareness (SSA) at the Unit Level: Increased SSA enabled by information sharing over the network allows units at the platoon level to focus more of their mental efforts on fighting the enemy and less on keeping track of their location and the location of the rest of their unit. This increase in SSA has the potential, yet unmeasured, to result in increased survivability and lethality.[7]

Value of Increased SSA in Increasing OPTEMPO: Increases in SSA have allowed units at the platoon and company level to remain in tactical march formations longer, utilizing the speed of these formations to increase the operational tempo of battle. On several occasions, this increased operational tempo has allowed blue forces to surprise opposition forces and gain tactical advantages. Before the increase in situational awareness enabled by information sharing, units had to move into attack formation earlier to avoid surprise contact with the enemy and to conserve combat power and greater lethality.

Value of Increased SA in Maintaining Force Ratio: At the brigade and division level, increased situational awareness has allowed to commanders to leave forces in contact longer with the enemy. Increased situational awareness of blue and red forces allows commanders to develop a better real time understanding of the status and disposition of their forces, of red forces, and of force ratios. This increased battlespace awareness gives them the confidence to allow units to stay in contact longer with the enemy, resulting in increased combat power.

Value of Increased SA in Reducing Risk: Both at Fort Hood and the National Training Center (NTC) units at the company and battalion level have reportedly been able to conduct more complex tactical maneuvers with less risk as a result of increased situation awareness enabled by the network. For example, the double-envelopment maneuver, during which the central part of a ground force retreats or stays in place while the flanks advance to gain superior position and to envelop an enemy force, has proven easier to execute, with less risk. Similarly, passage of lines in which a major new force passes through a blocking force to occupy a key position has been executed more successfully at the NTC.

Value of Increased SA to Battle Command: Finally, networking the force has reportedly assisted a division commander by giving him the increased situation awareness needed to maneuver against an adversary. In this case, the commander was able to monitor an enemy column on his right that was maneuvering. Rather than being forced to deploy his forces and alter his scheme of maneuver to engage the force, he was able to monitor its progress as it moved into an area not vital to him. Knowing its location, he was able to first complete his primary mission by executing his original plan, then maneuver his forces to defeat the now-isolated enemy force.

Division Capstone Exercise— Phase 1

Phase I of the Division Capstone Exercise (DCX) was conducted in April 2001, at Fort Irwin, California. The purpose of this DCX I was to demonstrate and assess the 4th Infantry Division's Mechanized and Aviation Brigades' ability to contribute decisively to III Corps' land campaign counteroffensive capability in the context of a Joint exercise. One of the principle goals of the DCX was the demonstration and assessment of the increased combat power enabled by multiple ongoing digitization and equipment modernization programs. The DCX Blue Force (BLUEFOR) was composed of approximately 7,500 soldiers in two Brigade Combat Teams (BCTs) consisting of elements of the 2nd and 4th Brigades of the 4th Infantry Division, F-16s and A-10s equipped with the Situational Awareness Data Link from the Arizona National Guard for close-air support, and Joint Surveillance Target Attack Radar System. The DCX Opposing Force (OPFOR) consisted of NTC OPFOR elements fighting with their traditional home field advantage.

The 2nd BCT comprised a heavy force of three battalions (three companies each) equipped with state-of-the-art M1A2 SEP Abrams tanks and M2A3 Bradley fighting vehicles. One of the battalions was composed of three tank companies; another, two tank companies and one infantry fighting vehicle company; and the third, one tank company and two infantry fighting vehicle companies. Supporting the operations of the 2nd BCT were an M109A6 Paladin field artillery battalion, an engineer battalion, and a forward support battalion. The 4th BCT consisted of a battalion minus (two companies) of AH-64D Longbow Apache attack helicopters, a battalion minus of UH-60 Blackhawk helicopters, two troops of OH-58D Kiowa Warrior reconnaissance helicopters, and an aviation support battalion. The DCX also evaluated several new brigade organizational structures, including a brigade reconnaissance troop (BRT), three company battalions, forward support battalions, and organic engineer assets.[8]

Leveraging the dramatic increases in situational awareness enabled by the networking of the digitized force, the 4th Infantry Division's two BCTs were more agile, had greater precision and were able to be more adaptable in changing situations. Although official TRADOC findings from the Division Capstone Exercise—Phase I have not yet been released an initial quick look analysis—highlighted the ability of the Blue Force (BLUEFOR) to significantly improve its warfighting effectiveness by creating and leveraging an information advantage.[9] Qualitative insights support key elements of the Network Centric Warfare hypotheses. In comparison with the Task Force XXI AWE, the BLUEFOR that participated in DCX Phase I appeared to have developed and mastered new TTP which enabled it to leverage the power of the network to significantly increase its warfighting effectiveness.

Information sharing enabled by the network enabled the BLUEFOR to develop a superior information position and exploit this position to gain overmatching shared situational awareness. The BLUEFOR was able to leverage this situational awareness advantage to rapidly focus lethality with precision maneuver (M1A2 Abrahms, M2A3 Bradley, AH-64D Apache) and conduct successful, simultaneous, and decisive operations. The ability of the BLUEFOR to share information over the network and develop a common operational picture had a dramatic impact across all echelons of command. A key theme was increased speed. Vignettes which illustrate the employment of Network Centric Warfare concepts are presented below.

Horizontal Information Sharing—Increased Speed—Improved OODA Performance—Distributed OODA—Armor to Artillery

An M1A2SEP tank identified an OPFOR Armed Personnel Carrier (a BMP) during a company raid at 5 KM away. Since the BMP was beyond direct fire range, the tank used its far target location capability to precisely locate the target (OBSERVE) by lazing and selecting the call for fire template from the reports menu on the FBCB2. The tank commander then digitally relayed a Call for Fire to the company FIST-V and it was relayed to the DS firing battery (ORIENT, DECIDE).

The initial fires achieved a firepower kill on the BMP and the following fire for effect resulted in a catastrophic kill (ACT).

This far target location capability gives the M1A2SEP tank and the M2A3 Bradley an exceptional capability to call for accurate, lethal fires out to the limit of their ability to laze.

Factors Contributing to Reduced OPFOR Situational Awareness

Three key factors to contributed to the BLUEFOR's ability to develop a situational awareness overmatch over the OPFOR. The BLUEFOR's rapid scheme of maneuver combined with their ability to conduct bold maneuvers at night in difficult terrain significantly reduced OPFORs capability to develop situational awareness on the status and disposition of the BLUEFOR. The OPFOR stated that it was only able to develop a 70 percent solution of BN TF areas rather than the normal 6-digit grid coordinate for vehicles that they had been able to develop during previous rotations. This situation was exacerbated by blue's ability in several instances to attrit the OPFORs reconnaissance capabilities. During one operational situation the BCT's UAV spotted an OPFOR Division Reconnaissance Company moving south. The BCT's Military Intelligence Company relayed this information via FM radio to a Mechanized Company in close proximity that was escorting a rearward movement of refugees. The Mechanized Company moved to and destroyed seven of the OPFOR's Division Reconnaissance Vehicles. This is an excellent example of self-synchronization enabled by networking the force.

Benefit of Multi-Echelon Command and Control (Collaborative OODA)

The shared operational picture enabled the Division Tactical Command Center to assist the 2nd BCT in performing command and control (Collaborative OODA). At one point during the BLUEFOR's maneuver, the command and control element manning the Division Tactical Command Center was able to use the common operational picture to rapidly identify a situation where elements of a Battalion Combat Team (BCT) were out of position and provide guidance to reposition the BCT. In this specific situation, the 2nd BCT was in the execution phase of clearing CMF forces/movement to contact up to a Phase Line. One of the operators from the Fire Support Element observed that several tanks from the 2nd BCT had moved north of the Phase Line (the limit of advance for the 2nd BCT, with the exception of the BRT (Brigade Reconnaissance Troop). This instance of rapid collaborative command and control enabled 2nd BCT's forces to relocate themselves to support the Commander's operational plan.

Shared Knowledge of Commander's Intent

Digitization and networking has enabled staffs to share information on commanders' intent to the lowest levels, resulting in the capability of the 4th Infantry Division (ID) to develop a shared knowledge of commander's intent (in the cognitive domain). During the initial movement of the 4th ID, the staff was able to understand the commander's intent to the lowest level. Specialist and privates monitoring the battle were able to understand the big picture. Enlisted soldiers were able to monitor the battlefield and develop a better understanding of what was going on in the battlefield.

Sensors (UAV, JSTARS) Contributions to Increased SA

The BLUEFOR's ability to employ organic sensors and exploit sensors such as JSTARS has helped commanders visualize the enemy and terrain and to see and strike quickly before the enemy was prepared or when he did not expect to be attacked. Particularly lethal in the deep attack where AH-64 D Apache helicopters teamed with UAVs to form hunter-killer teams. On several occasions, the Commander was able use UAVs to identify OPFOR forces and then maneuver attack helicopters to engage and perform shaping operations prior to contact OPFOR engagement of BLUEFOR. In another operational situation, increased SA of BLUEFOR enabled the ADC-M to rapidly conduct interdicting fires with MLRS and F-16 CAS sorties. In the course of the air strikes the pilots identified approximately 45 vehicles in a ravine. The ADC-M then ordered additional strikes on these vehicles before releasing the sorties to 2nd BCT control.

Benefit of Improved Situational Awareness to Logistics and Support

Greater situational awareness played a key role in increasing the effectiveness of logistics and support units and creating a force multiplier. For example, the increased situational available to logistics and support units improved their ability to find and fix broken and disabled platforms and increased velocity of repair. The net result was increased combat effectiveness of the 2nd BCT. An additional demonstrated benefit of total asset visibility and anticipatory logistics was the ability to employ modular and tailorable approaches that resulted in smaller logistics footprints and reduced lift requirements.

Operational Benefits

The anticipated operational benefits of digitization and networking for maneuver are portrayed in Figure 84. While the gains in information quality, information sharing, situation awareness, shared awareness, collaboration, and synchronization must be estimated, the data on planning speed, mission outcomes, calls for fire, and force lethality are consistent with the hypothesized patterns.

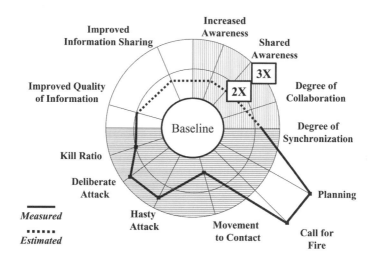

Figure 84. Maneuver

Counter Special Operation Forces Mission

One of the most significant examples of the power of network-centric operations to date occurred when Fleet Battle Experiment (FBE) Delta was conducted by the U.S. Navy in conjunction with Combined Forces Command Korea. This command faces major warfighting challenges in three mission areas: Counter Fire, Counter Special Operations Forces (CSOF), and Theater Air and Missile Defense. Each of these missions was addressed in Fleet Battle Experiment Delta, conducted in October 1998 in conjunction with Exercise Foal Eagle '98, an annual joint and combined exercise sponsored by Combined Forces Command Korea.

In this experiment, the results with the greatest operational significance were generated in the CSOF mission area, where the seemingly intractable problem of countering hundreds of North Korean special operations boats (a CSOF mission) was dealt with on a timeline previously not thought possible.

In this experiment, elements of the Army's 2nd Infantry Division, AH-64 Apache Helicopter Squadrons from the 6th Combat Air Brigade, a range of Navy and Marine Corps units, and a Maritime Air Support Operations Center were networked via a wide area network to form a land-sea engagement network. Operating on this network were two command and control applications, the Army Deep Attack Operations Control System (ADOCS) and the Land Attack Warfare System (LAWS), a prototype software application derived from ADOCS. The use of these applications enabled all elements to share information and develop a common operational picture, resulting in improved coordination between Naval, Air, and Ground Component Commanders.[10] The ability of networked forces to develop a common operational picture enabled them to simultaneously achieve a very high level of shared situational awareness that, when combined with new tactics, techniques, and procedures, allowed these forces to synchronize their efforts from the bottom up to achieve dramatically increased combat power and to accomplish their mission in half the time required with traditional platform-centric operations.[11]

The empirical results from FBE Delta and subsequent modeling and simulation are as follows:[12]

- Average Decision Cycle Time was reduced from 43 to 23 minutes.

- Average Mission Timeline (command and control time plus operational time) was cut in half.

- Shooter effectiveness (kills per shot) was increased 50 percent.

- Assets scrambled was decreased by 15 percent.

- Leakers (special operations vessels that passed through the engagement zone to their operational destinations) were decreased by a factor of 10.

The qualitative implications of this experiment are very impressive. The network increased shared awareness to such an extent that the units involved could self-synchronize. That process increased operational tempo and shooter effectiveness, which in turn, saved assets. The consequences of an order of magnitude decrease in the number of special operations vessels reaching their intended destination is also of significance in that it would greatly simplify the defensive operations on the South Korean peninsula.

CINCPAC, Admiral Blair, highlighted the implications of FBE Delta during a speech at WEST 2001 in San Diego in January of 2001, where he stated:

> *FBE Delta unlocked the potential combat power that was latent in the joint task force, but had been wasted due to segmentation of the battlespace.*[13]

Theater Air and Missile Defense (TAMD)

In the TAMD mission, networking was shown to enable a force to significantly improve its warfighting capability. In this mission, sensors play a key role in generating battlespace awareness (Figure 85). Stand-alone radar sensors, such as the E-2 Hawkeye, and sensors on weapons platforms, such as AEGIS radar, detect and track objects ranging from aircraft to cruise and ballistic missiles. When these sensors are employed in the battleforce in stand-alone (platform) mode, scattering effects and environmental factors can combine and interact to degrade both detection and tracking quality. These problems are most serious against stressing targets, those characterized by high speed and/or low observables. This may mean loss of track continuity, unacceptably slow track convergence, or even failure to initiate a track against certain types of objects. The net result is poor situational awareness in the cognitive domain, which can significantly impact mission performance. Operational performance can be significantly increased through employment of the Network Centric Warfare concepts of Sensor and Engagement Grids. These concepts are operationalized with the Cooperative Engagement Capability.

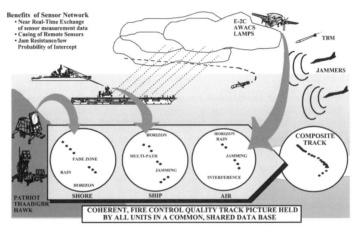

Figure 85. Theater Air and Missile Defense Process

The Cooperative Engagement Capability (CEC) networks battle force sensors and enables the force to share information and improve its information position by overcoming the limits of individual sensors. CEC is a unique battle force sensor netting system consisting of cooperative engagement processors and data distribution systems on all cooperating units: ship, air, and shore. Utilizing highly advanced data transfer and processing techniques, CEC is able to integrate the air defense sensors of CEC equipped surface ships, aircraft, and land sites into a single composite network that generates fire control quality information (An example of increased information richness enabled by increased reach). CEC integrates the radar and IFF measurements on each platform and distributes the measurement data to all cooperating units. This provides each cooperating unit an identical, real-time air picture based on all CEC battle force sensors. CEC's greater track accuracy, better identification (lower uncertainty), and decreased time to achieve a given level of track accuracy combine to give battle force commanders a higher quality of information to work with. Equally important, detection ranges are extended, which allows further time compression and more rapid achievement of engagement quality battlespace awareness, as portrayed in Figure 86.

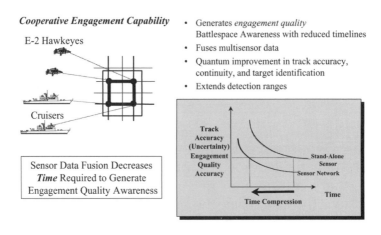

Figure 86. Impact of Network Centric TAMD

Tactical decision making in the TAMD arena is improved directly by facilitating key decisions: which target to engage, when to engage it, and which shooter and which weapon should be used to maximize the probability of a kill. New TTPs are emerging to allow commanders to exploit the significantly improved battlespace awareness that can be achieved in this mission area through the employment of CEC. For example, Fire of Remote Data, in which a shooter engages a target it never acquires directly, but rather uses information provided by an external sensor, holds considerable promise for improving battle force asset utilization and TAMD mission effectiveness.[14]

Strike

Network centric concepts are also enabling new warfighting capabilities in the strike arena. During Operation Allied Force, the Kosovo air operation, U.S. and coalition air crews flew more than 36,000 sorties in support of a wide range of missions. Numerous firsts were achieved, including the first combat deployment of the B-2 Spirit and the largest employment of Unmanned Aerial Vehicles (UAV) in history. The UAVs were employed as stand-alone platforms and in conjunction with a wide range of other ISR (intelligence, surveillance, and reconnaissance) assets, including JSTARS, RIVET JOINT, AWACS, U-2, and other coalition and sister-service sensors.[15]

One of the major challenges faced by Allied Air Forces was finding, fixing, targeting, and engaging mobile ground targets. JSTARS operators, who had been extremely successful during Operation Desert Shield/ Desert Storm at deterring and tracking moving ground targets in the desert, found that weather, terrain, and other factors made it very difficult to identify and classify possible targets in Kosovo. Moreover, Forward Air Controllers (FAC) and strike aircraft found it difficult to identify small, mobile targets from 15,000 feet (the approximate altitude needed to reduce vulnerability to surface-to-air missiles in the theater) with their onboard sensors.[16]

In an attempt to overcome some of these obstacles, the kill chain was networked, as is illustrated in Figure 87. This linked sensors, analysts, decisionmakers, and shooters in new ways. The Predator (UAV) operated by the U.S. Air Force's 11th Reconnaissance Squadron was deployed to Tuzla Air Base in Bosnia. Imagery from the UAV was transmitted via SATCOM to a ground station in England, then via fiber optic cable to a processing facility in the United States. The processed information was then transmitted to the Washington, D.C., area, where it was up-linked to a Global Broadcasting System (GBS) satellite and transmitted back into the operational theater. This information was received at the CAOC (Combined Air Operations Center) in Vicenza, Italy. Targeting information was then communicated to controllers aboard an airborne command and control aircraft, which then provided it to the FAC. The FAC, in turn, provided the information to strike aircraft in accordance with established TTPs.

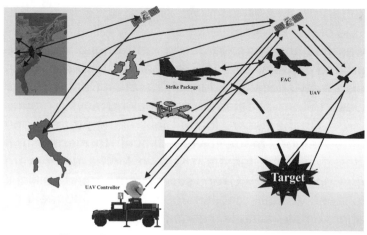

Figure 87. Strike: Networking the Kill Chain

The employment of this network-centric kill chain enabled the force to significantly improve its information position as portrayed in Figure 88. By employing reach-back linkages to generate analysis and targeting decisions promptly, the delays that often enable mobile targets to avoid detection and attack were minimized.

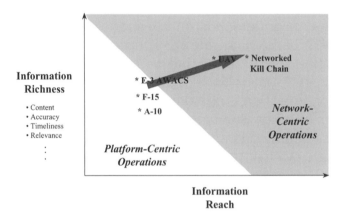

Figure 88. Strike: Improved Information Position

Split-Based Operations

The final example, taken from Air Force experimentation efforts in Expeditionary Force Experiments (EFX) 98 and 99, highlights the power of collaboration and synchronization. During these experiments, the Air Force, supported by joint and coalition partners, explored more than 50 concepts, processes, and technology initiatives.[17]

Employing networks to increase combat power was central to both EFXs. A core theme was distributed operations. During JEFX 99, a forward CAOC, which consisted of approximately 300 people, was linked to and supported from a much larger, CONUS-based Operations Support Center (OSC).[18] The operational benefits of this organizational arrangement are significant. In the past the forward deployed organization employed 1,500 to 2,000 people as shown in Figure 89. These personnel needed to be taken into theater along with the equipment they needed to do their jobs. This forward organization also makes major demands on transportation (reportedly 10 C-17 loads) during the early phases of an operation, reducing the lift available to move shooters and essential logistics to support them into the theater. Not only Air Force personnel and material, but also those of other Services must compete for this lift. Hence, learning to network the force at this level and operate with an effective and efficient split-based CAOC will pay major dividends in combat power. While the Air Force has reported key operational challenges based on the JEFX experience, they have also made a commitment to operationalizing this concept.

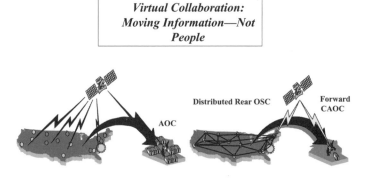

Figure 89. Split-Based Operations

The ability to use networks to increase situational awareness in control aircraft, fighters, bombers, and other support aircraft (fuel tankers, jammers, etc.) has also been a core theme during both EFX 98 and JEFX 99. At its limits, this will enable us to launch long-range bombers from secure bases in CONUS and to either provide specific targets or update target lists while they are en route to the operational theater.[19] This can improve our ability to conduct effective and efficient air operations in any corner of the planet.

Observations and Conclusions

These examples clearly demonstrate that U.S. and Allied Armed Forces are beginning to understand the potential power of network-centric concepts, approaches, and capabilities. The evidence shows that, enabled by a sufficient degree of connectivity and interoperability, a variety of organizations have achieved increased awareness, created shared awareness, and leveraged this by developing new ways of doing business that increase the speed of command and the tempo of operations.

While the breadth of these mission areas is impressive, it should be pointed out that this evidence comes from a limited portion of the mission spectrum. As noted in the introduction to this volume, efforts to develop evidence about Information Age Warfare remain scattered or hit and miss, rather than focused or systematic. The fact that few of these examples actually reach across whole mission areas and that none of them really deal with the complexity inherent in Joint Task Force, operational level missions, or the Operations Other Than War (OOTW) that dominate practical experience today, mean that a great deal of research remains to be done.

However, the importance of this evidence should not be minimized. The significant improvement in combat power documented here lends considerable weight to the central hypotheses of Network Centric Warfare. Clearly, there is a benefit to employing a more systematic approach to organizing research; collecting evidence in operations, exercises, experiments, and demonstrations; and in assessing that evidence. In addition, there is also a compelling benefit to going beyond traditional combat to explore the full range of command and control concepts enabled by Information Age technologies.

---

[1]AFTTP 3-3.4: Combat Aircraft Fundamentals—F-15. The Air Force Tactics, Techniques, and Procedures (AFTTP) 3-3 series publications are the primary aircraft fundamental reference document for the USAF. This series provides a comprehensive, single-source document containing fundamental employment procedures and techniques necessary to accomplish various missions.

[2]*JTIDS Operational Special Project (OSP) Report to Congress*, Mission Area Director for Information Dominance, Office of the Secretary of the Air Force for Acquisition (Washington, DC: Headquarters U.S. Air Force, December 1997).

[3]*Ibid.*

[4]This information and the subsequent discussions of Task Force XXI AWE and the U.S. Army Division AWE are drawn from Robert C. Holcomb, "Some Lessons Learned While Digitizing the Battlefield," *Proceedings of the Battlefield Systems International Conference* (London, 1998).

[5]BG William L. Bond, USA, *Army Digitization Overview*, Briefing to Dr. Jacques Gansler, USD (A&T), at the Pentagon (Washington, DC, May 20, 1998).

[6]*Exercise Big Picture 1 Final Report*, Defense Evaluation and Research Agency (October 1997).

[7]This section is drawn from *NCW—Emerging Lessons Learned from the First Digital Division*, Presentation by COL (Ret) Fred Stein at conference on "Network Centric Warfare: Missions, Needs, Opportunities, and Challenges" (Washington, DC, October 21-22, 1999).

[8]Scott R. Gourley, "Redefining War," *Military Information Technology*, Volume 5, Issue 5 (June 2001), pp. 22-23.

[9]Frederick P. Stein, Presentation on "DCX-Phase I" to *Network Centric Warfare...Understanding the Operations and Systems of the Revolution in Military Affairs*, AFCEA Course 513 (Washington, DC, June 1, 2001).

[10]*Fleet Battle Experiment Delta Quick Look Report* (Newport, RI: Maritime Battle Center, Naval Warfare Development Command, November 2, 1998).

[11]VADM Arthur K. Cebrowski, Written testimony to hearing on Defense Information Superiority and Information Assurance— Entering 21st Centery, held by the House Armed Services Committee, Subcommittee on Military Procurement (February 23, 1999).

[12]*Fleet Battle Experiment Delta Quick Look Report* (Newport, RI: Maritime Battle Center, Navy Warfare Development Command, November 2, 1998). *An Assessment of IT-21 Warfighting Value-Added* (March 1, 1999).

[13]ADM Dennis Blair, CINCPAC, remarks during keynote address at WEST 2001 (San Diego, CA, January 23, 2001).

[14]"The Cooperative Engagement Capability," *Johns Hopkins APL Technical Digest 16, 4* (1995), pp. 377-396.

[15]Earl H. Tilford, "Operation Allied Force and the Role of Air Power," *Parameters* (Vol. 29, Issue 4, Winter 1999/2000), pp. 24-38. Jacques de Lestapis, *DRONES, UAVs Widely Used in Kosovo Operations*, http://www.periscope.ucg.com/docs/special/archive/special-199907011327.shtml

[16]David A. Fulghum, "DARPA Tackles Kosovo Problems," *Aviation Week and Space Technology* (August 2, 1999), pp. 55-56. John A. Tirpik, "Short's View of the Air Campaign," *Air Force Magazine* (September 1999), pp. 43-47.

[17]EFX Fact Sheet, http://efx.acc.af.mil/factsheet.htm, accessed September 17, 1998.

[18]*JEFX 99 Final Report*, http://jefxlink.langley.af.mil/milfinal99/main.htm, accessed January 1, 2000.

[19]*Ibid.*

CHAPTER 11

Assessment and the Way Ahead

In the previous chapter, we reviewed some of the emerging evidence that supports the central hypothesis of the new mental model. In this chapter, this evidence will be put into an overall context and its implications for DoD will be discussed.

There is good news, better news, and cause for concern.

The good news is that we are on to something big. Information Superiority and Network Centric Warfare concepts really do translate into combat effectiveness (in the case of combat and improved operational capabilities in non-traditional military missions). The value of the new mental model has been demonstrated. In addition, the power and importance of coevolving mission capability packages is being confirmed and attests to the importance of our emerging program of experimentation. This is clearly good news.

The very good news is that we have hardly scratched the surface of what is possible. We have been, for the most part, focused on relatively safe extensions of current concepts and processes. We have only had a very limited amount of pair-wise interoperability to work with. In other words, we have only just begun to explore the possibilities. However, there are ominous clouds on the horizon.

Infostructure

First, our infostructure (information infrastructure) will not be ready to support network-centric operations. We are becoming more dependent on a fragile and vulnerable infostructure. Interoperability problems persist within each of the Services and in the Joint arena. The increasing importance of coalition operations is still not adequately mirrored by an effort to achieve coalition interoperability. In short, there is a disconnect between the future concepts being developed and the planned reality of the infostructure in the same time frame. Finally, there are a number of significant impediments to progress.

There are many impediments that are affecting our ability to make progress on the development and fielding of a secure, reliable, and interoperable infostructure. Progress on this infostructure is being constrained by:

• Lack of infostructure visibility;

• Inadequate requirements definition;

• Program-centric planning;

• Insufficient integration;

• Delays in deploying technology; and

• Lack of Joint systems commands and labs.

Infostructure Disconnects

Our future warfighting concepts, built upon leveraging Information Superiority, are predicated upon the existence of a secure, reliable, and interoperable infostructure. We are, in effect, banking on an infostructure, one that will not be there unless we focus our collective efforts on making it happen. We have the right vision, but this vision is not yet being translated into reality. We need to pay the entry fee! If not, our future will be full of shortfalls including:

- Lack of connectivity

- Interoperability

- Bandwidth to the last mile

- Security

- Mobility

- Survivability

Vulnerabilities

The DoD infostructure is funded and managed not as a single integrated entity, but as a collection or federation of systems and capabilities that belong to the Services and Defense Agencies. As the Defense Planning Guidance observes, a vulnerability or deficiency in one of these systems affects everyone. In other words, a risk accepted by one is a risk imposed upon all.

As we adopt a network-centric approach, it is important that we pay more attention to the end-to-end functionality of our federation of systems and capabilities to ensure that the resulting infostructure is indeed robust, secure, and has the functionality to satisfy our information needs.

Innovation and Concept Development

The conditions that result in our focusing on safe ideas, if not altered, will inhibit truly innovative ideas! Progress on design of information-enabled mission capability packages is being constrained by:

- Lack of understanding of future capabilities;

- Lack of information-enabled experimental venues; and

- Lack of harvesting of small experiments.

Fielding of New Capabilities

Our current policies and processes make it difficult to move rapidly from idea to demonstration to fielded capability. Progress on the balanced development of mission capability packages is being constrained by:

- Continued emphasis on platform-centric investments and concepts;

- Separate and unequal treatment of mission capability package elements;

- Lack of mission capability package visibility and analysis; and

- Failure to work the nexus between organizations, doctrine, and information technology.

These factors, taken together, highlight the fact that our approach to innovation and the infostructure that supports it is not up to the challenge. We can no longer afford to continue business as usual. For if we do, we will forgo many of the most promising opportunities of the Information Age. We need to rethink our approach to innovation, experimentation, and the process of coevolving DoD infostructure mission capability packages, build in a higher degree of infostructure visibility, and take steps to ensure the emergence of a coherent infostructure.

Given the evidence to date about the importance of the coevolution of mission capability packages, we must address existing impediments to coevolution and provide sufficient degrees of freedom for them to reach their full potential.

In addition to suffering a large opportunity loss, we are exposing ourselves to an unnecessary risk. The risk is that our fragile and vulnerable infostructure will be degraded in times of need, with particularly severe adverse mission consequences.

The Way Ahead

This is a time for deeds, not words. The early evidence is in, and our strategic vector is clear. Only the details remain to be worked out. This is, of course, the refrain of the visionary and the optimist. The pessimist frets that "the devil is in the details." The truth, of course, lies somewhere in between. Progress will depend upon much more than having a strategic vector. It will also depend on the development of an understanding of the basics—

how to create shared awareness, effective collaboration, and meaningful synchronization in the battlespace.

At the most fundamental level, we need to ensure that our information systems, including the human processes involved in them, are reengineered to ensure interoperability. This has been a growing priority and point of emphasis for DoD policy over the past decade. The idea of a Joint Technical Architecture emerged as a recognition that not everything was being born joint and that some means to ensure interoperability was needed. The subsequent stream of C4ISR Support Plans and the 1999 assignment of Title 10 responsibility for interoperability to the DoD CIO have resulted in several formal policy initiatives to further that goal. At this writing the need for genuine reengineering processes focused on interoperability has become obvious. This is essential if the set of legacy and new systems is to be federated in ways that makes sense not only from the perspective of communications engineers, but also in terms of the military mission packages needed to move toward Information Superiority.

Thus, DoD's journey into the future is inextricably tied to progress in our understanding of how to create and leverage Information Superiority. This is not simply a technical problem that, once solved, can be packaged in a "black box" and deployed. Rather, it is a constant quest involving an ongoing dialogue among technologists, scientists, analysts, and operators. In order to make meaningful progress, we need to keep up with a continuous stream of ever-increasing capabilities that advances in technology provide, and also to keep ahead of our adversaries in bringing what are essential commercially available capabilities to the battlefield. We must do the following:

- Create the conditions needed to spawn innovative ideas;

- Provide venues and tools to rigorously test new ideas and theories;

- Streamline the process that transforms validated ideas into military capability; and

- Conduct systematic research in areas that are needed to improve our understanding of the new mental model.

Innovation can be inhibited in a number of ways, including the existence of institutional disincentives that actually punish departures from the accepted view. It will not be enough simply to reduce these barriers. A climate for innovation is necessary, but not sufficient. In order to think of innovative ways of accomplishing a task, individuals must be aware of the possibilities that exist and have some level of understanding about what Information Superiority and Network Centric Warfare are all about.

While there is a fair amount written on the Information Age and its possibilities, the overwhelming bulk of that material is devoted to experiences and opportunities found in the private sector. While these certainly provide food for thought, a parallel literature, dealing with the full spectrum of military operations and national security challenges and opportunities, needs to be encouraged and made widely available.

To make these ideas more concrete, DoD needs to be committed to providing a critical mass of secure interoperability that allows individuals throughout DoD to experience opportunities to network, and a level of sophisticated information-related capabilities that allows those individuals to understand the nature of their information needs. Appropriate education and training, along with an organizational focus on thinking about exploiting these opportunities to rethink the way military operations are done, complete the package.

As sciences go, the science of information is very much in its infancy. DoD needs to greatly increase the attention paid to research in the ways individuals and teams use and share information, develop awareness and shared awareness, and make decisions. New approaches to command and control merit a significant investment in research that goes far beyond the technology orientation of the past. Models and simulations (M&S), at their best, capture our understanding of the processes they represent. Currently the best of these are woefully inadequate in their representations of information flows, information uses, and the relationships that affect decisions. They also do a very poor job of representing the characteristics and impacts of command and control processes on military operations. While the developers of M&S could do a lot better than they are currently doing, much of this lack of M&S capability can be related to a more systemic lack of understanding of informational, cognitive, and organizational processes. The existence of appropriate and useful metrics is part of the problem and why we, in this book, devoted so much of our attention to this subject. Clearly much more needs to be done.

Metrics are key because they form the bridge between reality and theory. They are the conduits of feedback from field experiments to researchers. They are the essence of the communication between analysts and the users of analysis. They focus us. Metrics for the Information Superiority value chain must continue to evolve over time from trial, error, and inspiration. Without the heavy spade work of applying metrics to the problems at hand, progress will not occur. To aid this process, we must insist on the collection and sharing of quantitative data from all of our research, experiments, field trials, and actual operations.

Of course, what one collects is more important than how much is collected. The primitives and related metrics presented in this book are intended to provide a sound starting point. They are an attempt to measure what is important, not just what can be readily measured. We recognize that in the beginning it will be hard for individual projects to do a satisfactory job of measuring all of the Information Superiority attributes of interest. However, if we stick to it, things will improve. Someday these concepts will be routinely measured and contribute to increasing our understanding of the value of information and the power of networking. Meanwhile, the databases resulting from serious projects will provide a foundation for future work and innovation.

New venues are needed to facilitate the exploration and testing of ideas. These will serve as test ranges for Information Superiority and Network Centric Warfare. Like weapons ranges, these venues need to provide an environment that supports the collection of quality data and the control of selected independent variables. Expert teams of analysts are needed to help ensure that the tests are well conceived, well conducted, and well analyzed. A wide assortment of models, simulations, and analytic tools are needed to complete the picture. Unlike test ranges, however, these venues need to be able to provide trained personnel who can assume a variety of roles so that it is the ideas that are being tested, not the individual participants.

Finally, there needs to be an improved process that focuses the research on the high priority areas and develops synergy from individual research and experimental efforts. This process needs to bring together traditional science and technology programs with experimentation and command and control related research. Above all, it must help us gain insight into the human elements—cognitive processes, organizational dynamics, the role of perceptions, doctrine, and training.

Implications

Earlier we asserted that the strategic vector was clear. *Joint Vision 2020* provides such a vector. The implications for concepts of operation, command and control, force structure, and supporting processes are profound. With the realization that the details still need to evolve out of a systemic effort to understand and experiment with new ways of doing business that are designed to leverage the value of information and the power of networking, we conclude this book with a discussion of the implications of the Information Age for military operations and organizations. These implications should be thought of as hypotheses that need to be tested, refined, and retested as part of a process designed to coevolve future mission capability packages.

We will move to a networked force. Entities will be conceived and built net-ready to connect, with the presumption that they will increasingly depend upon non-organic information for their preferred mode of operations. Battlespace entities will not only receive information, but will be suppliers of information as well. Hierarchical flows of information will be streamlined, and peer-to-peer flows greatly increased. Interoperability will migrate down to lower and lower echelons. Security will be designed and built in. We will think differently about what we acquire and deploy. The infostructure or Global Information Grid will be seen as an enterprise capability and will be treated as such in the Planning, Programming, and Budgeting System process and will be managed as such.

We will stop thinking about systems and start thinking about systems of systems or federations of systems. The concept of software maintenance will be replaced with the concept of evolutionary systems. Thus, we will no longer buy a system, but set aside a funding wedge to develop and evolve a specific set of capabilities. Testing will evolve to a continuous activity that supports coevolution, and its focus will shift from system testing to end-to-end testing.

Achieving the right balance among the various elements of a mission capability package (concepts of operation and concepts for command and control, information flows, organization, and doctrine, education and training, weapons, logistics, and supporting systems) will be our primary challenge. Our current preoccupation with material will slowly change to a holistic approach. Information and its transformation into knowledge in support of distributed decisionmaking will emerge as a unifying theme that connects the elements of the mission capability package. We will invest in mission capability packages and portfolios designed to deliver them (not individual programs). The concept of tooth-to-tail will be replaced by a focus on the efficient delivery of effects.

A new understanding of command and control, based upon dynamically managing complex adaptive systems, will replace traditional cyclical approaches to command and control, resulting in the ultimate merging of the planning and execution processes. Information operations will quickly move from fantasy to reality, with IO capabilities being integrated into operations all across the conflict spectrum.

But most important of all, tradition will not be thought of as doing things the way they have always been done, but as a continuing effort to strive for increased understanding and innovation.

Understanding and Doing

The nature of the relationship between understanding and doing is a function of: a) the rate of change, and b) the degree to which the change or innovation is sustaining or disruptive.

During times when the rate of change is comparable to or slower than an organization's ability to adopt new technology and methods, understanding and doing are sequential activities. Lessons are learned from doing, better ways of doing things are developed, perfected, turned into doctrine, and then reflected in training and exercises.

The time required for an organization to change depends, of course, on the nature of the change. The introduction of new technology that improves upon, but does not significantly alter, existing processes and organizations (innovations that sustain the status quo) can be accomplished far more quickly than changes that are discontinuous and disturb established relationships, alter the distribution of responsibilities, and require new ways of thinking about accomplishing the tasks at hand. On the other hand, when the change involves not only the introduction of new technology, but also changes in the concept of operation along with associated changes in organization and doctrine, then the time required to adapt increases.

At this point in our history, the U.S. military faces the most stressing situation possible—one in which the rate of change exceeds our ability to change rapidly enough to keep pace, even if we were to choose merely to keep abreast of technological advances. But we cannot settle for just keeping pace with advancing technology because information technologies are by their very nature disruptive. They alter the environment in which organizations operate and demand that we coevolve concepts of operation and associated mission capability packages. This last statement warrants further explanation as to why the introduction of advanced information technologies demand disruptive change in military organizations.

Simply put, military organizations operate the way they do today because traditional concepts of command and control have evolved over time to deal with the fog and friction of war. Hence, military organizations have adapted themselves to operating in a world dominated by uncertainty and a lack of ability to rapidly and accurately convey information effectively across the force. Thus, in order to avoid blunders and to marshal mass, deliberate centralized planning became the mainstay of military operations. The planning processes that have evolved serve not only to convey commander's intent, but also to convey detailed information regarding the situation and what to do about it.

Advanced information technologies alter the fundamental assumptions upon which traditional command and control concepts, organization, and doctrine are based. These technologies create a vastly improved ability to develop and share situation awareness as well as enabling distributed collaborative environments. Thus, they fundamentally alter the information that can be provided to individuals throughout the organization. These technologies also provide us with the ability to increase the precision, stand-off ranges, and rate of fire of our weapons. In addition, offensive IO capabilities are and will continue to be added to our arsenal.

The proliferation of militarily significant information technologies will be far quicker and more pervasive than the proliferation of previous generations of military technologies since they are, in essence, driven by the commercial marketplace. This will result in a very dynamic threat environment, which, in and of itself, is disruptive. Potential adversaries may be highly motivated and/or better positioned to leap ahead by using new technologies in new ways. Their embracing disruptive innovation would have serious implications for the continuity of the threat environment.

Thus, we in DoD are faced with a situation in which our ability to change falls short of our need to change— and with a traditional linear process to technology insertion and change, which has become unsatisfactory and will only grow more unsatisfactory over time.

Clearly, we need to rethink not only our approach to C2, but also how we innovate, how we acquire technologies, and how we train. We believe that the solution lies in understanding the critical roles of innovation and real experimentation, the need to coevolve mission capability packages, and the need for a DoD-wide infostructure that is robust, reliable, interoperative, and secure.

As we begin the 21st century, we have an opportunity to step back and consider fundamental changes in the way we invest in, acquire, equip, and train our forces. The dynamics of the Information Age will punish us if we do not adapt to a new way of doing business. The brave and dedicated members of our armed forces deserve better. They deserve a DoD that can take full advantage of the opportunities afforded by Information Age concepts and technologies. To give them this, we must be prepared to endure disruptive change.

Bibliography

AFTTP 3-3.4: Combat Aircraft Fundamentals—F-15. The Air Force Tactics, Techniques, and Procedures (AFTTP) 3-3 series publications are the primary aircraft fundamental reference document for the USAF.

Alberts, David S., and Richard E. Hayes. *Command Arrangements for Peace Operations.* Washington, DC: National Defense University Press, May 1995.

Alberts, David S. "C2I Assessment: A Proposed Methodology." *Proceedings for Quantitative Assessment of the Utility of Command and Control System.* McLean, VA: MITRE Corporation, 1980.

Alberts, David S., John J. Garstka, and Frederick P. Stein. "Implications for MCPs." *Network Centric Warfare: Developing and Leveraging Information Superiority*, 2nd Edition (Revised). Washington, DC: CCRP Publication Series, 1999.

Alberts, David S. *The Unintended Consequences of Information Age Technologies: Avoiding the Pitfalls, Seizing the Initiative.* Washington, DC: National Defense University Press, 1996.

An Assessment of IT-21 Warfighting Value-Added (March 1, 1999).

Blair, ADM Dennis, USN, CINCPAC. Remarks during keynote address at WEST 2001. San Diego, CA, January 23, 2001.

Bond, BG William L., USA. *Army Digitization Overview*. Briefing to Dr. Jacques Gansler, USD (A&T), at the Pentagon. Washington, DC, May 20, 1998.

Boyd, Col. John R., USAF. "A Discourse on Winning and Losing." A collection of unpublished briefings and essays. Maxwell AFB, AL: Air University Library, 1976-1992. http://www.belisarius.com/modern_business_strategy/boyd/essence/eowl_frameset.htm (January 1996).

Boyd, Col. John R., USAF. *Patterns of Conflict*. Unpublished Lecture, 1977.

Brown, Anthony Cave. *Body Guard of Lies.* New York: Bantam Books, 1976.

Builder, C.H., S.C. Bankes, and R. Nordin. *Command Concepts: A Theory Derived from the Practice of Command and Control.* RAND Corp. MR-775-OSD, 1999.

Cebrowski, Vadm Arthur K., USN, and John J. Gartska. "Network Centric Warfare: Its Origin and Future." *Proceedings of the Naval Institute* 124:1 (January, 1998).

Cebrowski, VADM Arthur K., USN. Written testimony to hearing on Defense Information Superiority and Information Assurance—Entering 21st Century, held by the House Armed Services Committee, Subcommittee on Military Procurement, February 23, 1999.

Cohen, William S., Secretary of Defense. *Annual Defense Report to the President and the Congress*, Washington, DC, January 2001.

Czerwinski, Thomas J. *Coping with the Bounds: Speculations on Nonlinearity in Military Affairs*. Washington, DC: National Defense University Press, 1998.

Darilek, Richard , Walter Perry, Jerome Bracken, John Gordon, and Brian Nichiporuk. *Measures of Effectiveness for the Information-Age Army*. Santa Monica, CA and Arlington, VA: RAND, 2001.

de Lestapis, Jacques. *DRONES, UAVs Widely Used in Kosovo Operations*, http://www.periscope.ucg.com/docs/special/archive/special-199907011327.shtml

Druzhinin, V.V. "Concept, Algorithm, Decision (A Soviet View)." Moscow: Translated and published under auspices of USAF, USGPO, Volume 6 of "Soviet Military Thought," Series Stock # 0870-00344, 1972.

EFX Fact Sheet, http://efx.acc.af.mil/factsheet.htm, accessed September 17, 1998.

Evans, Phillip B., and Thomas S. Wurster. "Strategy and the New Economics of Information," *Harvard Business Review* (September-October 1997).

Exercise Big Picture 1 Final Report. Defense Evaluation and Research Agency, October 1997.

Fleet Battle Experiment Delta Quick Look Report. Newport, RI: Maritime Battle Center, Navy Warfare Development Command, November 2, 1998.

Fulghum, David A. "DARPA Tackles Kosovo Problems," *Aviation Week and Space Technology* (August 2, 1999).

Garstka, John J. "Network Centric Warfare: An Overview of Emerging Theory," *PHALANX* (December 2000).

Gourley, Scott R. "Redefining War." *Military Information Technology*, 5:5 (June 2001).

Hayes, Richard E., T.A. Hollis, Richard L. Layton, W.A. Ross, and J.W.S. Spoor. "Enhancements to the Army Command and Control Evaluation System Task 1 Final Report." FT Leavenworth, KS: U.S. Army Research Institute, 1993.

Headquarters Effectiveness Assessment Tool "HEAT" User's Manual. McLean, VA: Defense Systems, Inc., 1984.

Headquarters Effectiveness Program Summary Task 002. Prepared for C3 Architecture and Mission Analysis, Planning, and Systems Integration Directorate, Defense Communications Agency. McLean, VA: Defense Systems, Inc., September 1983.

Herman, Mark. *Measuring the Effects of Network-Centric Warfare*, Vol. 1. Technical report prepared for the Director of Net Assessment, Office of the Secretary of Defense. McLean, VA: Booz Allen & Hamilton, April 28, 1999.

Holcomb, Robert C. "Some Lessons Learned While Digitizing the Battlefield." *Proceedings of the Battlefield Systems International Conference* (London, 1998).

Information Superiority: Making the Joint Vision Happen. Office of the Assistant Secretary of Defense (Command, Control, Communications, & Intelligence). Washington, DC: Pentagon, November, 2000.

INSS Strategic Forum. Number 14, January 1995, http://www.ndu.edu/inss/strforum/z1405.html

Janis, Irving L. *Groupthink: Psychological Studies of Decisions and Fiascoes.* Boston: Houghton Mifflin, 1982.

JEFX 99 Final Report. Http://jefxlink.langley.af.mil/milfinal99/main.htm, accessed January 1, 2000.

Joint Vision 2020. Chairman of the Joint Chiefs of Staff, Director for Strategic Plans and Policy, J5, Strategy Division. Washington, DC: U.S. Government Printing Office, June 2000.

JTIDS Operational Special Project (OSP) Report to Congress. Mission Area Director for Information Dominance, Office of the Secretary of the Air Force for Acquisition. Washington, DC: Headquarters U.S. Air Force, December 1997.

Keegan, John. *Six Armies in Normandy: From D-Day to the Liberation of Paris*. New York: Penguin Books, 1982.

Kirzl, John E., Diana G. Buck, and Jonathan K. Sander. "Operationalizing the AIAA COBP for Joint C2 Experimentation." *Proceedings of the Command and Control Research and Technology Symposium 2000*. Monterey, CA: June 2000.

Klein, Gary. *Sources of Power*. Cambridge: MIT Press, 1998.

Loughran, Julia, and Marcy Stahl. "The DICE Experiment: Creating and Evaluating a Web-based Collaboration Environment for Interagency Training." Vienna, VA: ThoughtLink, Inc., May 2000. http://www.thoughtlink.com/publications/TLI-DICE99Abstract.htm

Merriam-Webster's Collegiate Dictionary, Tenth Edition. Springfield, MA: Merriam-Webster, Inc., 1995.

NCW—Emerging Lessons Learned from the First Digital Division. Presentation by COL (Ret) Fred Stein at the conference on "Network Centric Warfare: Missions, Needs, Opportunities, and Challenges." Washington, DC, October 21-22, 1999.

Noble, David, Diana Buck, and Jim Yeargain. "Metrics for Evaluation of Cognitive-Based Collaboration Tools." *Proceedings of the 6th International Command and Control Research and Technology Symposium 2001.* Annapolis, MD: June 2001.

Perrow, Charles. *Normal Accidents: Living with High Risk Technologies.* New York: Basic Books, Inc., 1984.

Spinney, Franklin C. "Genghis John." *Proceedings of the U.S. Naval Institute*, July 1997.

Stein, Frederick P. Presentation on "DCX-Phase I" to *Network Centric Warfare…Understanding the Operations and Systems of the Revolution in Military Affairs.* AFCEA Course 513, Washington, DC, June 1, 2001.

"Systematic Assessment of C2 Effectiveness and Its Determinants." *Proceedings of the 1994 Symposium on Command and Control Research and Decision Aids* (June 1994).

Tanner, Robert G. *Stonewall in the Valley: Thomas J. "Stonewall" Jackson's Shenandoah Valley Campaign, Spring 1862.* Mechanicsville: Stackpole Books, 1996.

"The Cooperative Engagement Capability." *Johns Hopkins APL Technical Digest* 16:4 (1995).

Tilford, Earl H. "Operation Allied Force and the Role of Air Power." *Parameters* 29:4 (Winter 1999/2000).

Tirpik, John A. "Short's View of the Air Campaign." *Air Force Magazine* (September 1999).

About the Authors

Dr. Alberts is currently the Director of Research, OASD (NII). Prior to this he was the Director, Advanced Concepts, Technologies, and Information Strategies (ACTIS), Deputy Director of the Institute for National Strategic Studies, and the executive agent for DoD's Command and Control Research Program. This included responsibility for the Center for Advanced Concepts and Technology (ACT) and the School of Information Warfare and Strategy (SIWS) at the National Defense University. He has more than 25 years of experience developing and introducing leading-edge technology into private and public sector organizations. This extensive applied experience is augmented by a distinguished academic career in computer science, operations research, and Government service in senior policy and management positions. Dr. Alberts' experience includes serving as a CEO for a high-technology firm specializing in the design and development of large, state-of-the-art computer systems (including expert, investigative, intelligence, information, and command and control systems) in both Government and industry. He has also led organizations engaged in research and analysis of command and control system performance and related contributions to operational missions. Dr. Alberts has had policy responsibility for corporate computer and telecommunications capabilities, facilities, and experimental laboratories. His responsibilities have also included management of research aimed at enhancing the usefulness of systems, extending their productive life, and the development of improved methods for evaluating the contributions that systems make to organizational functions. Dr. Alberts frequently contributes to Government task forces and workshops on systems acquisition, command and control, and systems evaluation.

John J. Garstka is currently the Assistant Director, Concepts and Operations, Office of Force Transformation, Office of the Secretary of Defense. Mr. Garstka is a recognized thought leader and globally respected international speaker in the area of Network Centric Warfare. In addition to coauthoring *Network Centric Warfare: Its Origin and Future*, which appeared in proceedings of the Naval Institute in January 1998, he is also the coauthor of *Network Centric Warfare: Developing and Leveraging Information Superiority*, which was first published in May 1999. This book has been reprinted by leading IT companies and translated into three different languages. Prior to joining the Office of Force Transformation, Mr. Garstka was the Chief Technology Officer in the Joint Staff, Directorate for Command, Control, Computer and Communications (C4) Systems. In this capacity he played a key role in the development and conceptualization of Network Centric Warfare and was the Joint Staff lead for DoD's *NCW Report to Congress*, July 2001. Previously Mr. Garstka was a Senior Systems Engineer with Cambridge Research Associates, where he had responsibility for leading consulting engagements with commercial and Government customers and in his career he served as an officer in the United States Air Force Space and Missile Center.

As President and founder of Evidence Based Research, Inc., Dr. Hayes specializes in multidisciplinary analyses of command and control, intelligence, and national security issues; the identification of opportunities to improve support to decisionmakers in the defense and intelligence communities; the design and development of systems to provide that support; and the criticism, test, and evaluation of systems and procedures that provide such support. His areas of expertise include crisis management; political-military issues; research methods; experimental design; simulation and modeling; test and evaluation; military command, control, communication, and intelligence (NII); and decision-aiding systems. Since coming to Washington in 1974, Dr. Hayes has established himself as a leader in bringing the systematic use of evidence and the knowledge base of the social sciences into play in support of decisionmakers in the national security community, domestic agencies, and major corporations. He has initiated several programs of research and lines of business that achieved national attention and many others that directly influenced policy development in client organizations.

Dr. Signori is Vice President and Senior Scientist at Evidence Based Research, Inc., where he spearheads initiatives and research related to C4ISR and Force Transformation. Prior to joining EBR, Dr. Signori served as a research leader at the RAND Corporation; The Special Assistant to the Director of DARPA for Warfare Information Technology; Deputy Director of DISA, Vice Manager of the National Communication System, Associate Director for Engineering and Technology, and Director of the Center for Command and Control and Communication Systems at the Defense Information

Systems Agency (DISA); The Associate Director of the Systems Evaluation Division at the Institute of Defense Analyses (IDA). Dr. Signori received his B.S. in electrical engineering from Worcester Polytechnic Institute in 1964 and his M.S. and Ph.D. in electrical engineering from Michigan State University in 1968. He served as a Captain in the Army Signal Corps from 1968 to 1970.

Catalog of CCRP Publications

Coalition Command and Control*
(Maurer, 1994)

Peace operations differ in significant ways from traditional combat missions. As a result of these unique
characteristics, command arrangements become far
more complex. The stress on command and control
arrangements and systems is further exacerbated by
the mission's increased political sensitivity.

The Mesh and the Net
(Libicki, 1994)

Considers the continuous revolution in information
technology as it can be applied to warfare in terms
of capturing more information (mesh) and how people and their machines can be connected (net).

Command Arrangements for
Peace Operations
(Alberts & Hayes, 1995)

By almost any measure, the U.S. experience shows
that traditional C2 concepts, approaches, and doctrine are not particularly well suited for peace
operations. This book (1) explores the reasons for
this, (2) examines alternative command arrangement
approaches, and (3) describes the attributes of effective command arrangements.

Standards: The Rough Road to the Common Byte
(Libicki, 1995)

The inability of computers to "talk" to one another is a major problem, especially for today's high technology military forces. This study by the Center for Advanced Command Concepts and Technology looks at the growing but confusing body of information technology standards. Among other problems, it discovers a persistent divergence between the perspectives of the commercial user and those of the government.

What Is Information Warfare?*
(Libicki, 1995)

Is Information Warfare a nascent, perhaps embryonic art, or simply the newest version of a time-honored feature of warfare? Is it a new form of conflict that owes its existence to the burgeoning global information infrastructure, or an old one whose origin lies in the wetware of the human brain but has been given new life by the Information Age? Is it a unified field or opportunistic assemblage?

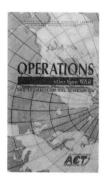

Operations Other Than War*
(Alberts & Hayes, 1995)

This report documents the fourth in a series of workshops and roundtables organized by the INSS Center for Advanced Concepts and Technology (ACT). The workshop sought insights into the process of determining what technologies are required for OOTW. The group also examined the complexities of introducing relevant technologies and discussed general and specific OOTW technologies and devices.

Dominant Battlespace Knowledge
(Johnson & Libicki, 1996)

The papers collected here address the most critical aspects of that problem—to wit: If the United States develops the means to acquire dominant battlespace knowledge, how might that affect the way it goes to war, the circumstances under which force can and will be used, the purposes for its employment, and the resulting alterations of the global geomilitary environment?

Interagency and Political-Military Dimensions of Peace Operations: Haiti - A Case Study
(Hayes & Wheatley, 1996)

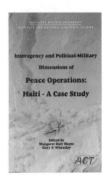

This report documents the fifth in a series of workshops and roundtables organized by the INSS Center for Advanced Concepts and Technology (ACT). Widely regarded as an operation that "went right," Haiti offered an opportunity to explore interagency relations in an operation close to home that had high visibility and a greater degree of interagency civilian-military coordination and planning than the other operations examined to date.

The Unintended Consequences of the Information Age*
(Alberts, 1996)

The purpose of this analysis is to identify a strategy for introducing and using Information Age technologies that accomplishes two things: first, the identification and avoidance of adverse unintended consequences associated with the introduction and utilization of information technologies; and second, the ability to recognize and capitalize on unexpected opportunities.

Joint Training for Information Managers*
(Maxwell, 1996)

This book proposes new ideas about joint training for information managers over Command, Control, Communications, Computers, and Intelligence (C4I) tactical and strategic levels. It suggests a substantially new way to approach the training of future communicators, grounding its argument in the realities of the fast-moving C4I technology.

Defensive Information Warfare*
(Alberts, 1996)

This overview of defensive information warfare is the result of an effort, undertaken at the request of the Deputy Secretary of Defense, to provide background material to participants in a series of interagency meetings to explore the nature of the problem and to identify areas of potential collaboration.

Command, Control, and the Common Defense
(Allard, 1996)

The author provides an unparalleled basis for assessing where we are and were we must go if we are to solve the joint and combined command and control challenges facing the U.S. military as it transitions into the 21st century.

Shock & Awe:
Achieving Rapid Dominance*
(Ullman & Wade, 1996)

The purpose of this book is to explore alternative concepts for structuring mission capability packages around which future U. S. military forces might be configured.

Information Age Anthology:
Volume I*
(Alberts & Papp, 1997)

In this first volume, we will examine some of the broader issues of the Information Age: what the Information Age is; how it affects commerce, business, and service; what it means for the government and the military; and how it affects international actors and the international system.

Complexity, Global Politics,
and National Security
(Alberts & Czerwinski, 1997)

The charge given by the President of the National Defense University and RAND leadership was threefold: (1) push the envelope; (2) emphasize the policy and strategic dimensions of national defense with the implications for complexity theory; and (3) get the best talent available in academe.

Target Bosnia: Integrating Information Activities in Peace Operations*
(Siegel, 1998)

This book examines the place of PI and PSYOP in peace operations through the prism of NATO operations in Bosnia-Herzegovina.

Coping with the Bounds*
(Czerwinski, 1998)

The theme of this work is that conventional, or linear, analysis alone is not sufficient to cope with today's and tomorrow's problems, just as it was not capable of solving yesterday's. Its aim is to convince us to augment our efforts with nonlinear insights, and its hope is to provide a basic understanding of what that involves.

Information Warfare and International Law*
(Greenberg, Goodman, & Soo Hoo, 1998)

The authors, members of the Project on Information Technology and International Security at Stanford University's Center for International Security and Arms Control, have surfaced and explored some profound issues that will shape the legal context within which information warfare may be waged and national information power exerted in the coming years.

Lessons From Bosnia:
The IFOR Experience*
(Wentz, 1998)

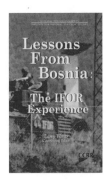

This book tells the story of the challenges faced and innovative actions taken by NATO and U.S. personnel to ensure that IFOR and Operation Joint Endeavor were military successes. A coherent C4ISR lessons learned story has been pieced together from firsthand experiences, interviews of key personnel, focused research, and analysis of lessons learned reports provided to the National Defense University team.

Doing Windows: Non-Traditional
Military Responses to Complex
Emergencies
(Hayes & Sands, 1999)

This book provides the final results of a project sponsored by the Joint Warfare Analysis Center. Our primary objective in this project was to examine how military operations can support the long-term objective of achieving civil stability and durable peace in states embroiled in complex emergencies.

Network Centric Warfare
(Alberts, Garstka, & Stein, 1999)

It is hoped that this book will contribute to the preparations for NCW in two ways. First, by articulating the nature of the characteristics of Network Centric Warfare. Second, by suggesting a process for developing mission capability packages designed to transform NCW concepts into operational capabilities.

Behind the Wizard's Curtain
(Krygiel, 1999)

There is still much to do and more to learn and understand about developing and fielding an effective and durable infostructure as a foundation for the 21st century. Without successfully fielding systems of systems, we will not be able to implement emerging concepts in adaptive and agile command and control, nor will we reap the potential benefits of Network Centric Warfare.

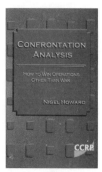

Confrontation Analysis: How to Win Operations Other Than War
(Howard, 1999)

A peace operations campaign (or operation other than war) should be seen as a linked sequence of confrontations, in contrast to a traditional, warfighting campaign, which is a linked sequence of battles. The objective in each confrontation is to bring about certain "compliant" behavior on the part of other parties, until in the end the campaign objective is reached. This is a state of sufficient compliance to enable the military to leave the theater.

Information Campaigns for Peace Operations
(Avruch, Narel, & Siegel, 2000)

In its broadest sense, this report asks whether the notion of struggles for control over information identifiable in situations of conflict also has relevance for situations of third-party conflict management—for peace operations.

Information Age Anthology:
Volume II*
(Alberts & Papp, 2000)

Is the Information Age bringing with it new challenges and threats, and if so, what are they? What sorts of dangers will these challenges and threats present? From where will they (and do they) come? Is information warfare a reality? This publication, Volume II of the Information Age Anthology, explores these questions and provides preliminary answers to some of them.

Information Age Anthology:
Volume III*
(Alberts & Papp, 2001)

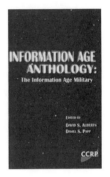

In what ways will wars and the military that fight them be different in the Information Age than in earlier ages? What will this mean for the U.S. military? In this third volume of the Information Age Anthology, we turn finally to the task of exploring answers to these simply stated, but vexing questions that provided the impetus for the first two volumes of the Information Age Anthology.

Understanding Information Age Warfare
(Alberts, Garstka, Hayes, & Signori, 2001)

This book presents an alternative to the deterministic and linear strategies of the planning modernization that are now an artifact of the Industrial Age. The approach being advocated here begins with the premise that adaptation to the Information Age centers around the ability of an organization or an individual to utilize information.

CCRP Publications

Information Age Transformation
(Alberts, 2002)

This book is the first in a new series of CCRP books that will focus on the Information Age transformation of the Department of Defense. Accordingly, it deals with the issues associated with a very large governmental institution, a set of formidable impediments, both internal and external, and the nature of the changes being brought about by Information Age concepts and technologies.

Code of Best Practice for Experimentation
(CCRP, 2002)

Experimentation is the lynch pin in the DoD's strategy for transformation. Without a properly focused, well-balanced, rigorously designed, and expertly conducted program of experimentation, the DoD will not be able to take full advantage of the opportunities that Information Age concepts and technologies offer.

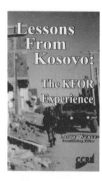

Lessons From Kosovo: The KFOR Experience
(Wentz, 2002)

Kosovo offered another unique opportunity for CCRP to conduct additional coalition C4ISR-focused research in the areas of coalition command and control, civil-military cooperation, information assurance, C4ISR interoperability, and information operations.

CCRP Publications

Power to the Edge: Command...Control... in the Information Age
(Alberts & Hayes, 2003)

Power to the Edge articulates the principles being used to provide the ubiquitous, secure, wideband network that people will trust and use, populate with high quality information, and use to develop shared awareness, collaborate effectively, and synchronize their actions.

Complexity Theory and Network Centric Warfare
(Moffat, 2003)

Professor Moffat articulates the mathematical models and equations that clearly demonstrate the relationship between warfare and the emergent behaviour of complex natural systems, as well as a means to calculate and assess the likely outcomes.

NATO Code of Best Practice for C2 Assessment
(2002)

To the extent that they can be achieved, significantly reduced levels of fog and friction offer an opportunity for the military to develop new concepts of operations, new organisational forms, and new approaches to command and control, as well as to the processes that support it. Analysts will be increasingly called upon to work in this new conceptual dimension in order to examine the impact of new information-related capabilities coupled with new ways of organising and operating.

Effects Based Operations
(Smith, 2003)

This third book of the Information Age Transformation Series speaks directly to what we are trying to accomplish on the "fields of battle" and argues for changes in the way we decide what effects we want to achieve and what means we will use to achieve them.

The Big Issue
(Potts, 2003)

This Occasional considers command and combat in the Information Age. It is an issue that takes us into the realms of the unknown. Defence thinkers everywhere are searching forward for the science and alchemy that will deliver operational success.